# THEORIES OF

# MACROCOSMS AND MICROCOSMS

## IN THE HISTORY OF PHILOSOPHY

BY

GEORGE PERRIGO CONGER, Ph.D.

NEW YORK / RUSSELL & RUSSELL

## AUTHOR'S NOTE

In the preparation of this monograph I have been especially helped by the suggestive criticisms of Professor F. J. E. Woodbridge and Professor John J. Coss, of Columbia University, and Professor Sterling P. Lamprecht, formerly of Columbia, now of the University of Illinois. Professor Richard Gottheil, of Columbia University, has given me some valuable references. Miss Margaret Jackson, of the University of Minnesota, has been of much assistance in reading the proofs.

GEORGE P. CONGER.

# CONTENTS

## INTRODUCTION

## CHAPTER I

### THE EMERGENCE OF MICROCOSMIC THEORIES IN THE GREEK AND GRÆCO-ROMAN WORLD

## CHAPTER II

### MICROCOSMIC THEORIES IN THEOLOGICAL TRADITIONS

## CHAPTER III

### MICROCOSMIC THEORIES IN EARLY MODERN REACTIONS FROM SCHOLASTICISM

## CHAPTER IV

### MICROCOSMIC THEORIES IN PHILOSOPHY FROM DESCARTES TO SPENCER

## CHAPTER VI

### CONCLUSION; GENERAL ESTIMATE OF MICROCOSMIC THEORIES

# INTRODUCTION

## i. Purpose and Title of this Study

The purpose of this monograph is to trace throughout the history of philosophy the motivations, contents and effects of a number of views which may be grouped under the title "Theories of Macrocosms and Microcosms." According to these theories, portions of the world which vary in size exhibit similarities in structures and processes, indicating that one portion imitates another or others on a different scale. Most prominent among the theories are those to the effect that man is a microcosm, or "little world," in one way or another epitomizing a macrocosm, or "great world"—*i. e.*, the universe, or some part thereof. At the outset it should be noted that the definition of the field of investigation is a matter of some difficulty—one is likely to conceive it in terms either too inclusive or too restricted. On the one hand, it may be urged that all philosophy is a discussion of the relations of man and the universe, and that every particular philosophy may be stated in terms of a comparison between the two; thus the field of investigation would be broadened to embrace the whole history of philosophy, and, if explored, would distort that history by presenting it as approached from one angle. On the other hand, one is likely to think of the subject solely with reference to man and the universe, neglecting related views such as the atomisms and monadisms, which deal specifically with portions of the universe apart from man. Any criterion which indicates an avoidance of both these extremes is difficult to formulate; but it may be said that, within the field of broader philosophical generalizations, it is the more special characteristic of the views with which we are concerned, that they base conclusions with reference to the nature of the universe and the relations of its parts, including man, to one another, upon parallelisms and analogies describing in more or less detail the structures and processes of those parts. These views attain their most pronounced development in the work of Fechner; in the works of other philosophers they range all the way from detailed parallelisms like those of the mediæval Jewish and Arabian thinkers to the great metaphysical generalizations of Descartes and Spinoza and the epistemological achievements of Kant.

While in the writings of these men last named and others of their kind there are often traces of a feeling of peculiar kinship between man and the universe, there is not the attempt at a descriptive parallelism indicating, point by point, that one portion of the universe imitates another or others on a smaller scale—which is the clearest mark of the group of views with which we are concerned, and to which the term "theories of macrocosms and microcosms" is here applied.[1]

## 2. TOPICAL AND GEOGRAPHICAL RESTRICTIONS

Since the subject-matter is closely related to that of a number of other philosophical topics, it is well to indicate briefly that, while no exact line can be drawn, this study is not primarily concerned with animistic projections, or "collective representations," in primitive societies; nor with forms of theism which maintain, uncritically, that man is the image of God; nor, as partially indicated above, with systems of speculative metaphysics which trace the operation of highly abstract principles throughout the world or portions of it; nor with any form of the copy-theory of ideas; nor with metaphors and poetic expressions.

There is also a geographical restriction; for, although similar theories are found elsewhere, our consideration is usually confined to the philosophies of the Mediterranean and Atlantic regions.

## 3. DERIVATION OF TERMS

The words "macrocosm" and "microcosm," which are found in Latin, French, German, Italian and English forms, are equivalents for the inferred Greek term μακρὸς κόσμος,[2] "great world," and the early Greek term μικρὸς κόσμος, "little world." Possibly the adjective μακρός was first intended to refer to the long duration of the universe as compared with man.[2] Aristotle, in place of this, uses a form of the adjective μέγας;[3] the word "Megacosmus" is found in Latin, and its equivalent sometimes in English. The term μικρὸς κόσμος has been ascribed, upon doubtful authority, to Democritus;[4] its first indisputable occurrence is in Aristotle.[3]

---

[1] In the following pages, the term "microcosmic theories," or "theories of epitomization," in the plural, is used to indicate the general field of investigation, while the term "microcosmic theory," in the singular, is used for the view that man, rather than any other portion of the universe, epitomizes the whole.

[2] *New Engl. Dict.*, "macrocosm."    [3] *Phys.* VIII, 2, 252 b.    [4] See below.

## 4. SUMMARY OF PREVIOUS WORKS IN THIS FIELD

1. *Meyer's Monograph.* Of previous works in this field, the only monograph is by Adolf Meyer—*Wesen und Geschichte der Theorie vom Mikro- und Makrokosmos*, in *Berner Studien zur Philosophie und ihrer Geschichte*, volume 25, pages 1 to 122 (1900). After a review which covers many of the historical theories, Meyer distinguishes four types— the mythological-physical, the psychical, the metaphysical, and the sociological.[1] In his final estimate they are all dismissed as lacking scientific confirmation and depending too much upon reasoning from analogy. Acknowledgment is due to this work as the pioneer in the field, but attention should be called to a number of defects, especially omissions.

2. *Chapters and Sections on Special Periods.* Several other works, some of which will be referred to later, contain chapters or sections on the history of these theories during special periods. C. A. Lobeck, in his famous *Aglaophamus* (Berlin, 1829), volume II, chapter IX, "De Macrocosmo et Microcosmo," discusses various obscure aspects of the theories in connection with the Greek mystery religions. A. Jellinek's edition of Joseph Ibn Zaddik's *Olam Katan* (*Der Mikrokosmos, Ein Beitrag zur Religionsphilosophie und Ethik. . .* Leipzig, 1854) contains an introduction with a section (4), giving a summary of the theory among Jewish writers. Jellinek thinks that the theory helps to explain some points otherwise difficult to interpret. B. Beer's review of the foregoing in Frankel's *Monatsschrift für Geschichte und Wissenschaft des Judentums*, volume III, pp. 159 ff., 197 ff. (1854), contains additional suggestions. F. Dieterici, referring to the theory as a "Jahrtausende beherrschende Gedanke,"[2] familiar in his day, divides the general introduction and resumé of his translations of the encyclopædic treatises of the mediæval Arabian Brethren of Sincerity (*Die Philosophie der Araber im IX-ten und X-ten Jahrhunderten. . .*, Books I and II—Berlin, 1875-6) into two parts, one entitled "Einleitung und Makrokosmos," and the other, "Der Mikrokosmos." L. Stein, who suggested the work of Meyer, has, in the first volume of his *Psychologie der Stoa* (*Berliner Studien für classische Philologie und Archæologie*, III, 1—1886), a supplement entitled "Mikro- und Makrokosmos der Stoa." He thinks that in the Stoa we have the first clearly expressed microcosmic theory and that as soon as it is established that a philosopher had the conception of man as a micro-

---

[1] p. 104.   [2] *Op. cit.*, vol. I, p. 162.

cosm, one is justified in supposing that wherever there are striking analogies between man and the world there is an intended reference to the theory. W. Windelband in his *History of Philosophy* (English translation by Tufts, New York, 1901) devotes a section (29) to the theory during the humanistic period. He says that the revival of this "Peripatetic-Stoic" [1] doctrine helped to offset other tendencies. There is a valuable article by I. Broydé in the *Jewish Encyclopædia*, vol. VIII, page 544 (1904), reviewing the development of the theory in Jewish philosophy. J. Kroll, in *Die Lehren des Hermes Trismegistos* (*Beiträge zur Geschichte der Philosophie des Mittelalters*, XII, 1—Münster, 1914), has a brief chapter on "Der Mensch als der μικρὸς κόσμος," noteworthy for some of its references.

*3. Briefer References.* Attempts, sometimes misleading, to deal with the history of the theory that man is a microcosm are made in paragraphs and footnotes of other works, some of which will also be cited later. In T. Gataker's edition of Marcus Aurelius's *De rebus suis* (1652), there is a note (on IV, 27), with quotations from ancient writers. S. Munk, in his translation of Maimonides's *Moreh Nebuchim* (*Le guide des égarés*, Paris, 1856) says that the theory has its source with Pythagoras and Plato rather than with Aristotle.[2] M. Joël, in *Ibn Gebirol's Bedeutung für die Geschichte der Philosophie* (a supplement to vol. I of *Beiträge zur Geschichte der Philosophie*—Breslau, 1876), says that the microcosmic theory is more influential in the Neo-Platonic philosophers than in Plato, but that the Arabians elaborated it most thoroughly.[3] P. E. M. Berthelot, in *Les origines d'alchimie* (Paris, 1885) says that the theory of correspondence between the parts of the macrocosm and the microcosm is of Babylonian origin.[4] J. Guttmann, in *Die Philosophie des Salomon Ibn Gabirol* (Göttingen, 1889), corrects Joël by tracing the expression for "microcosm" to Aristotle, and gives references to Jewish writers.[5] M. Steinschneider, in *Die Hebräischen Übersetzungen des Mittelalters* (Berlin, 1893), traces the theory through obscure Jewish sources which he thinks not dependent upon the Arabian Brethren.[6] M. Baumgartner, in his *Die Philosophie des Alanus de Insulis* (*in Beiträge zur Gesch. der Philos. des Mittelalt.*, II, Münster, 1898), p. 88, has a note with references, especially to twelfth-century sources. A. Bouché-Leclercq, in his *L'astrologie grecque* (Paris, 1899) devotes unusual care to the analysis of the theory. He says that practically every ancient system of philosophy

[1] P. 369.   [2] Note on I, 72.   [3] P. 29.   [4] P. 51.   [5] P. 117, n. 3.   [6] P. 997, n. 1.

contributed something to it; that the Neo-Pythagoreans, Orphics, Neo-Platonists, hermetics and Christian Platonists insisted most upon it; but that the theory was greatly misused in astrology. The modicum of truth in the theory, according to him, is that man, being able to conceive only the human, has made God or the gods in his own image, and therefore finds everywhere the analogies of which he is the unconscious and sole author.[1] S. Horovitz, in *Die Psychologie bei den judischen Religionsphilosophen des Mittelalters* (in *Jahresbericht des Judischen Theologischen Seminars zu Breslau*, 1900), follows Siebeck in ascribing the theory to Heraclitus and has a note with references, notably one to Xenophon.[2] M. De Wulf, in his *History of Mediæval Philosophy* (1900; English translation by Coffey, N. Y., 1909), says that Gundisallinus modified this "Alexandrian conception." [3] S. Karppe, in *Études sur l'origin et la nature du Zohar* (Paris, 1901), finds the theory, although not the term, in Plato, and says it was familiar among the Neo-Platonists from the time of Jamblichus, and known among the Neo-Pythagoreans, as well as in Philo.[4] F. Cumont, in *Les religions orientales dans le paganisme romain* (Paris, 1906), says that the theory goes back to an animistic doctrine of "sympathy" common to all primitive peoples.[5] D. Neumark, in his *Geschichte der judischen Philosophie des Mittelalters* (Berlin, 1907), says that the theory among the Greeks had a psychological (*i. e.*, an animistic) background, but that Plato, Aristotle and the Neo-Platonists did not work it out in detail as did the Arabians.[6] E. V. Arnold, in *Roman Stoicism* (Cambridge, 1911) says that the doctrine, of unknown antiquity, is apparently implied in Heraclitus.[7] E. Underhill, in *Mysticism* (New York, 1912), emphasizes the part which the theory has played in occult speculations.[8] R. M. Jones, in *Spiritual Reformers in the Sixteenth and Seventeenth Centuries* (London, 1914), calls attention to the many strains of thought—ancient Greek and Græco-Roman philosophy, mediæval mysticism, Persian astrology, Arabian philosophy, and the Jewish Cabala—which were blended in and with the theory at the period with which he deals.[9] E. O. von Lippmann, in his *Entstehung und Ausbreitung der Alchemie* (Berlin, 1919), thinks the theory bears witness to an oriental origin, and calls it a Babylonian idea,[10] the first clear expression of which is to be found in the later works of Plato.[11]

*4. References in Dictionaries and Encyclopædias.* Works of reference

[1] Pp. 77–78.   [2] Anmerkung 110.   [3] Eng. transl., p. 273.
[4] P. 452, n. 1.   [5] P. 207.   [6] Vol. I, pp. 61–62.   [7] P. 240.
[8] P. 191.   [9] P. 134.   [10] Pp. 196, 666.   [11] P. 188.

which, under the word "microcosm" or "macrocosm," contain useful citations and summaries are W. Fleming's *Vocabulary of Philosophy* (1857); Larousse's *Grand dictionnaire universel* (1874); Eisler's *Wörterbuch;* Baldwin's *Dictionary of Philosophy; The New English Dictionary.* Their wide variations show how fragmentary is investigation in this field. One of the most noteworthy of such articles is that in F. Mauthner's *Wörterbuch der Philosophie* (Leipzig, 1910; vol. II, pp. 88, ff.). He points out that the word "macrocosm" is artificial, probably constructed more for alliteration than for content, and that it would be more accurate to substitute the term "makranthropos" for it. He says the term "microcosm" is at bottom a mechanistic conception applied to man, while the term "makranthropos" is a panpsychic conception applied to the world. Of the two, the latter ascription, although not the term, is doubtless older. From the modern point of view the idea of a macrocosm is only a poetic fancy, and the conception of a microcosm only a mechanistic inversion of it.

# CHAPTER I

# THE EMERGENCE OF MICROCOSMIC THEORIES IN THE GREEK AND GRÆCO-ROMAN WORLD

## I. GREEK PHILOSOPHY PRIOR TO PLATO

1. *Methods Available for Reconstruction.* The elaborate collections and interpretations of quotations from early Greek philosophers are likely to give the impression that their thinking was cast in the form of philosophical systems, but such system as is found is often traceable to the collection and discussion rather than to the content of the fragments. In connection with the subject before us, however, two considerations help to fix the significance of the fragments. In the first place, we need not suppose that the world of these philosophers was as full of lacunæ as are their literary remains; and if it is ever justifiable to attempt the reconstruction of a "background" for early Greek philosophy, such a reconstruction is almost certain to indicate a place for the development of microcosmic theories. Thus, according to J. Burnet [1] and F. M. Cornford,[2] the word κόσμος was first applied to the order observed in human society, and afterward extended to the physical world. If this is the case, countless interests of the social group as opposed to the forces of nature would cause the two types of order to be distinguished—at first, perhaps, implicitly, in attitudes and practices, and at length explicitly by adjectives and phrases. But one need not follow Burnet or Cornford in detail; one can say in general, and in agreement with accepted views of social origins, that wherever a social group, with a limited supply of facts, begins to distinguish order in the physical environment with which their social order has to contend, the way is open for a natural development of microcosmic theories. That it was the individual, animal or man, which later, as order came to be distinguished in this case also, was regarded as preëminently the microcosm, is quite in accord with the fact that in other respects developing individuality tended to force social considerations into the background. In the second place, there are some passages in the

---

[1] *Early Greek Philosophy* (London, 1908), p. 32.
[2] *From Religion to Philosophy* (London, 1912), p. 53.

fragments which, especially when compared, appear to be of significance for microcosmic theories, even though great allowance has to be made for mutilations, uncritical transmission, and biased interpretations.

2. *Criticism of Certain Statements about Thales.* In the case of Thales, the meagre evidence is not convincing. A. Weber says that Thales held that the earth derives nourishment from the water surrounding it; [1] but this view is traceable not to a citation from Thales, but to a conjecture of Aristotle.[2] If Thales, reasoning from the behavior of magnetic stones,[3] taught that the cosmos is ἔμψυχος,[4] this is an instance of animistic, rather than of microcosmic theory.[5]

3. *Earliest Trace of Microcosmic Theory in Anaximenes.* The first instance of recognition of a similarity of structure and process in the universe and in man is found in a fragment ascribed to Anaximenes. As preserved by Stobæus,[6] it is as follows:

"Just as our soul which is air holds us together, so it is breath and air that encompasses the whole world."

On the basis of this fragment, C. Baeumker [7] and Meyer [8] have agreed that Anaximenes is to be credited practically with having founded the theory of macrocosm and microcosm. Burnet says that he was influenced by the analogy.[9]

4. *Related Views among the Pythagoreans.* It is obvious that the Pythagorean doctrine of numbers, implying basic resemblances in all things, might easily be elaborated into a theory of epitomizing relations. Nor is it strange that Pythagoras, who, according to several ancient writers, was the first to call the world by the term κόσμος,[10] should be interpreted in accordance with microcosmic theories.[11] But " Pythagoras " is the name of a corporation even more than of an individual; passages

---

[1] *History of Philosophy* (Eng. transl., Thilly, N. Y., 1908), p. 21.

[2] *Met.* I, 3, 983 b 21.       [3] *De An.*, I, 2, 405 a 19.       [4] Diog. Laert., I, vi, 27.

[5] *Cf.* R. D. Hicks, *Stoic and Epicurean* (N. Y., 1910), p. 20.

[6] Stob., *Eclogæ*, I, x, 12, ed. Meineke (Leipzig, 1860).

[7] *Das Problem der Materie in der Griechischen Philosophie* (Münster, 1890), p. 15.

[8] *Op. cit.*, p. 99.

[9] *Greek Philosophy*, Part I. *From Thales to Plato* (London, 1914), p. 25.

[10] E. Zeller, *History of Greek Philosophy*, Eng. transl. Alleyne (London, 1881), vol. I, p. 472, n. 2.

[11] Meyer, *op. cit.*, p. 6, "Menschliche Ordnung . . . weitet er makrokosmisch aus." On p. 7 Meyer says that Erdmann ascribes the germ of the theory to Pythagoras and the Pythagoreans; but Erdmann (*Grundriss der Geschichte der Philosophie*, 4te Auflage, Berlin, 1896, p. 32) ascribes it to Platonic circles.

such as may be cited from Photius [1] and other writers undoubtedly belong to later periods.[2] Some features of the later Pythagorean teachings were quite microcosmic—for example, the view that there was a process of inhalation, whereby breath was drawn into the heavens from outside; [3] that the κόσμος had a right side and a left side; [4] that the heavens constituted a body, of which the sun, moon, stars and heavenly elements formed the eyes and other members, "as in man"; [5] and a more curious theory, attributed to Philolaus,[6] that the brain, heart, navel and genital organs, with their functions, corresponded to or represented man, the animals, the plants, and the *ensemble*, respectively.

*5. Attempts to Construe Microcosmic Views in Heraclitus.* According to the Heraclitean fragments, there is continual flux in the world, particularly between opposing forces; [7] such a flux is also observable in man and human affairs; [8] and there are direct connections between the world process and the soul.[9] Thus all the elements necessary for the construction of a microcosmic theory are here; there is lacking only a definite word from Heraclitus, fitting them together. Burnet has attempted to bridge this gap; his attempt is more conspicuous than that of Meyer,[10] although resting upon the same general principles. Burnet develops the comparison between the world and man; he thinks that Heraclitus explains the former by the latter.[11]

"Night and day, summer and winter, alternate in the same way as sleep and waking, life and death, and . . . the explanation is to be found in the successive advances of the wet and the dry, the cold and the hot. . . . 'The way up and the way down are one and the same ' . . . for the microcosm and the macrocosm." [12]

E. V. Arnold thinks that

"The doctrine that man is a representation or reflection of the universe . . . seems to be clearly implied by the teaching of Heraclitus, in so far as he lays it down that both the universe and man are vivified and controlled by the Logos." [13]

---

[1] *Bibliothecon*, codex 249 (ed. Bekker, Berlin, 1824, II, 440-a).
[2] *Cf.* Lobeck, *op. cit.*, vol. II, pp. 918–920.
[3] *Cf.* Aristotle, *Phys.* IV, 6; 213 b.   [4] Stobæus, *Eclog.*, I, xv, 6.
[5] Epiphanius, *Advers. hæres.*, I (1), hær. 5, ord. 7; Migne, *Patr. Gr.*, vol. XLI, col. 205.
[6] H. Diels, *Fragmente der Vorsokratiker* (2nd edition, Berlin, 1906–10), vol. I, p. 244— Philolaus, frgt. 13.
[7] *Ibid.*, pp. 61 ff. Heraclitus, frgts. 10, 51, 59, 60, 76, 80, 90, 103, 126.
[8] *Ibid.*, frgts. 58, 88, 111.   [9] *Ibid.*, frgts. 36, 77.   [10] *Op. cit.*, p. 10.
[11] *Early Gr. Phil.*, p. 168.   [12] *Gr. Phil.* I, pp. 60, 61.   [13] *Rom. Stoicism*, p. 240.

Yet it must be remembered that all these views are made out of the fragments, rather than found in them. At one time it seemed possible that more definite evidence of microcosmic views might be obtained from Heraclitus. According to Meyer,[1] an attempt was made by P. Schuster, in a work called *Heraklit von Ephesus* (1873), to show that Heraclitus saw a parallelism between the universe and man. This work was recognized and cited by H. Siebeck,[2] but according to Meyer is unreliable, because it ascribes to Heraclitus the famous treatise *De diæta*. Gomperz ascribes this treatise to the Hippocratic school;[3] Diels prints part of it with the Heraclitean fragments as an "imitation";[4] Burnet calls it pseudo-Hippocratean, but thinks that part of it is "almost certainly of Heraclitean origin."[5] In the treatise one finds the characteristic Heraclitean doctrine of a periodic flux, especially an interaction of fire and water.[6] There is a more explicit comparison between the processes of nature and those of man.[7] The crucial passage, for the documentation of a definite microcosmic theory, runs:

"In a word, the fire has ordered everything in the body in its own way, (an) imitation of the Whole, (setting) small over against great and great over against small; the . . . belly . . . (having the) power of the sea, nourisher of living creatures . . . imitation of the earth, transforming all things falling upon it."[8]

If this passage could be proved to have come from Heraclitus, one would need no further evidence; but it is worked out in fantastic detail which suggests a later period and a commentator. In general, however, one may say that it is strange if a relation between various portions of his teachings which has been so clear to the commentators was missed by the master.

*6. Suggested Interpretation of Some Empedoclean Fragments.* The same remark, that a relation between doctrines which is so clear to others might well have been clear to their author, applies to Empedocles. One is tempted to surmise that just as Newton is said to have had his apple, so Empedocles had his "klepsydra"; for it may be noted that, just as air and

[1] *Op. cit.*, pp. 8, ff.
[2] *Geschichte der Psychologie* (Gotha, 1880), vol. I, p. 43.
[3] *Greek Thinkers*, Engl. transl. Magnus (London, 1901), vol. I, p. 286.
[4] *Fragmente*, vol. I, pp. 81 ff.
[5] *Early Gr. Phil.*, p. 167.
[6] *De diæta* 1, 3, quoted by Burnet, *Early Gr. Phil.*, p. 183, n. 1.
[7] *De diæta*, I, 6, ff. Diels, *Fragmente*, vol. I, pp. 81-2.
[8] *De diæta*, I, 10; Diels, p. 83.

water alternately penetrate the klepsydra,[1] so Love and Strife alternately penetrate the great Sphairos.[2] Again, the klepsydra illustrates the process of breathing.[1] And once more, although the fragments in this case are not so clear, one may say that the principle observed in the klepsydra is not altogether absent from what might be called Empedocles's psychology. The eye is equipped with pores,[3] recalling those which function in breathing and, also, the perforations of the klepsydra;[4] the fire has concealed itself in the interior of the eye, and comes out through the pores.[3] Empedocles may very well have seen this resemblance between the various processes mentioned; and if he did, the famous doctrine that "like perceives like"[5] may belong in a microcosmic setting rather than in that of a theory about the subjectivity of sense-data.[6] According to one of the fragments,[7] Empedocles declared that he had made an important discovery; Burnet implies that this discovery was in the nature of a microcosmic theory.[8] Weber speaks according to the spirit rather than the letter of the evidence when he says that according to Empedocles "man is the image of the Sphairos. The four radical elements are represented in him."[9]

7. *Alleged Influence of the Hippocratean Writings.* According to Burnet, the rise of medicine in the fifth century B. C. made biological arguments popular.[10] The dates of the Hippocratean treatises are not precisely known; but some of them may have been early enough to figure in this period. Besides the *De diæta*, there was one *On the Number Seven*, which Gomperz discusses in connection with this period. According to this, animals and plants have a constitution resembling that of the universe; the earth resembles the bones; the air, the flesh around them; the river waters, the blood, and so on.[11] Gomperz thinks that the theory of the microcosm was "a grand idea in itself," but "bound to lead to fanciful interpretations" and, then as later, "to darken rather than illumine the path of natural research."[12] In this case, the comparisons, carried to ludicrous extremes, were, according to Gomperz, calculated to produce a reaction, which, when it ensued, marked the dawn of Greek science.[13]

---

[1] Diels, *sub* Empedocles, frgt. 100.
[2] *Ibid.*, frgts. 17, 21, 22, 35. *Cf.* Burnet, *Gr. Phil.*, I, pp. 72–3.
[3] Diels, *Fragmente*—Empedocles, frgt. 84.    [4] *Ibid.*, frgt. 100.
[5] *Ibid.*, frgt. 109.
[6] *Cf.* Gomperz, *op. cit.*, vol. I, pp. 235–6.
[7] Diels, frgt. 17, lines 25–6.    [8] *Gr. Phil.*, I, p. 73.
[9] *Op. cit.*, p. 47.    [10] *Early Gr. Phil.* (1908), p. 49.
[11] Gomperz, *op. cit.*, vol. I, pp. 294–5.    [12] *Ibid.*, p. 289.    [13] *Ibid.*, p. 295.

Whatever truth there may be in this statement should not be allowed to obscure the fact that there were many other influences which were at work to produce a more empirical and matter-of-fact science among the Greeks.

*8. On the Ascription of the Term " Microcosm" to Democritus.* Before considering these other influences we turn to Democritus, who was at any rate Pre-Platonic by birth. It is easy to construct microcosmic theories in an atomism, just as it is in a number-philosophy—each atom may be regarded as an image of every other. But the evidence that Democritus held any microcosmic theory is very faulty. The assertion is made by David of Nerken, an Armenian philosopher who flourished about 490 A. D., that Democritus called man the microcosm; [1] but the assertion remains practically unsupported. [2]

*9. The Older Microcosmic Theories Eclipsed by Humanistic Interests at Athens.* According to Xenophon, Socrates once developed an argument from analogy to sustain an Anaxagorean view of the world-soul; in it, he pointed out some relations between the composition of the world and that of the human body, as well as between the larger soul and the human soul. [3] But—assuming that the Platonic writings have more of the pupil than of the teacher—the Athenians, in the brilliant period marked by the visits of the earlier Sophists, were more interested along other lines. It mattered little to them what might transpire in the world outside the city walls, or beyond the reach of city policies; the question of possible resemblance of the greater world to the lesser lost its importance. The Athenians were not merely skeptical; [4] they were preoccupied. The ancient views were left high and dry, or relegated to groups like the Pythagoreans. There seems to be no allusion to microcosmic theories in the great dramatists, nor even in the historians. Everything centers around social and political questions. Men laugh at Socrates for an alleged interest in meteorology. No one thinks of interpreting the saying of Protagoras, that man is the measure of all things, with any

---

[1] *Prolegomena,* chap. XII (*Commentaria in Aristotelem græca,* vol. 18—ed. A. Busse, Berlin, 1904). Diels, *Fragmente*—Democritus, frgt. 34. On the terms μέγας διάκοσμος and μικρὸς διάκοσμος, see Diels, Leucippus, frgt. 1; Diog. Laert IX, 45–49, in Diels, p. 357; Burnet, *Early Gr. Phil.* (1908), p. 381. *Cf.* Porphyry; Stob. *Flor.* XXI, 27.

[2] Democritus is credited with the saying that the wise man is at home in the whole cosmos (Diels, frgt. 247).

[3] *Memorabilia,* I, 4.

[4] *Cf.* Meyer, *op. cit.,* pp. 17, ff.

emphasis on the "all things." And, when Plato begins to write, even the theory of macrocosm and microcosm begins to take a sociological form.

*10. The Pre-Platonic Period in Retrospect.* Unless the late Pythagorean and Hippocratean writers can be called Pre-Platonic, the evidence does not allow us to ascribe microcosmic theories definitely and explicitly to any of these thinkers, except Anaximenes, and in his case the one fragment is hardly sufficient for the foundation of a theory. But much of the evidence in the cases of Heraclitus and Empedocles points in the direction of a theory. When one considers not merely the literary evidence, but also the general conditions out of which philosophy, in common with other features of early civilization, developed, the probability is strengthened that microcosmic theories were familiar to the Greek thinkers who preceded Plato.[1]

## 2. The Writings of Plato and Aristotle

*1. Functions of Microcosmic Theories in Plato.* The interests of Plato were so varied that his works defy systematization in accordance with any one of them. In the dialogues in which the life of Socrates is dramatized, or those in which Plato displays his flashes of poetic genius, or those in which, attempting to answer the questions raised by the Sophists he strikes hither and thither in search of precise ethical and logical definitions, there is no trace of theories of epitomization. But wherever Plato the philosopher appears, to answer questions which Plato the dramatist has suggested or Plato—if not Socrates—the dialectician has elaborated; wherever, that is, Plato's work begins to be systematic and constructive, there, without using the term, he employs one or another of the microcosmic theories. It is always naïve—the work of a man who is trying to be systematic, but who is obliged to draw largely on his imagination for materials; and it is often obscured by his use of myth and allegory. It is chiefly apparent in his political, ethical, and cosmological views.

*2. Plato's Parallelism between Man and the State.* In the *Republic* there is the familiar comparison between the tripartite ideal state and the tripartite individual soul—to the effect that justice, in individual character, consists in a hierarchical relationship between reason, enthusiasms and appetites; and, in the state, in a similar relationship between the ruling, military, and producing classes.[2] Plato realizes, however, that

---

[1] *Cf.* references to passages in Philo, Macrobius, Galen and Chalcidius, below.

[2] *Republic*, 434–435, 441, 580 D, E. Since the Greeks, the northern barbarians, and the Phœnicians exhibited the qualities of the three classes, respectively, Plato's tri-

the relationship between individual and state is not so simple as it appears from this parallelism. His conception is not merely structural, that of an individual soul considered as a combination of three qualities and a state considered as a combination of three social classes; his conception is also, and even predominantly, what we may call functional, that of a comparison between what might now be termed individual and social psychology. In this latter aspect of his doctrine, the facts become conspicuous that the state gets its qualities and habits from the individuals which make it up,[1] and that individuals, in turn, partake of the qualities of the states in which they live.[2] But these structural and functional aspects are not regarded as out of all relation to one another; for it is said that the members of various classes in the state will manifest individual qualities which, in the scale of qualities, are comparable to the positions of those classes in the state.[3] There are some other indications, too, of Plato's interest in questions of structure, traceable in his comparisons of a troubled city and a diseased organism,[4] and in the curious prototype of later organismic theories, found in the *Laws*, according to which the city is to be compared to a trunk, the younger guardians to eyes, and the old men to a memory.[5] On the whole we may say that in his political philosophy Plato used structural comparisons to render more articulate those recommendations upon which he was intent; but it must be remembered that his chief interest here was not a biological parallelism, but a psychological description; not organism, but organization.

3. *Plato's Cosmology.*   The complicated machinery of the *Timæus* contains so many wheels within wheels that it lends itself easily to microcosmic interpretations. One must note, however, that some of the processes of imitation which it portrays are those by which, in accordance with the Platonic doctrine, the created and visible world forms a copy of an uncreated world (whatever Plato may have meant by this) and its contents.[6] The visible universe is thus "most like" its original;[6] it is spherical[7] and self-sufficient—it has no use for eyes, or breathing apparatus, or food from outside.[8] The visible universe is composed of the

partite division and parallelism might be extended to include a larger instance. Plato says (576 C), "As state is to state in virtue and happiness, man is to man."

[1] *Republic*, 435 E, 544 D, E.
[2] *Ibid.*, 441 C, D, 576 C, 577 D.
[3] *Ibid.*, 431 B–D, 433 C.
[4] *Republic*, 462 C, D, 464 B, 556 E; *Laws*, 628 D, 636 A, 735 D, 829 A, 906 C, 945 C.
[5] *Laws*, 964 D—965 A.   [6] *Timæus*, 30 C.   [7] *Ibid.*, 33 B.   [8] *Ibid.*, 33 C, D.

world-soul [1] and the world-body.[2] The world-soul is composed of "the Same," "the Other," and an intermediate "Essence" [1]—thus exhibiting a tripartite division, which may or may not have been meant to recall that of the individual soul in the *Republic*.[3] Within the world-body there are four kinds of beings, copies of those in the uncreated world [4]—these four kinds of beings are, first, the gods or stars, and then the animals of the air, water, and land, respectively [5]—perhaps designed to suggest the four elements. The gods, or stars, are shaped like the All, and are thus circular.[5] Among these the earth is included.[6] The animals of the air, water and land were created by the gods, who in forming man imitated the shape of the universe in the formation of the head,[7] and localized in the body the tripartite division of the soul.[8] Of the physiological processes, the movement of the blood, which is enclosed within the animal "as if under a sky," imitates the periodic processes of the universe.[9] Moreover, man should learn to imitate the harmonies of the universe, as the way to health and happiness.[10] Some passages in other dialogues are similar to portions of the *Timæus;* for instance, part of the myth of the charioteer in the *Phædrus*,[11] the curious speech of Aristophanes in the *Symposium*,[12] the story of the creation in the *Statesman*,[13] and the comparison of the movements of the heavens and those of the mind,[14] as well as the question raised about the body and soul of the sun,[15] in the *Laws*. The *Timæus* does not stand quite alone among the dialogues; its apparent isolation is due to the fact that Plato, like so many other Athenians, was not primarily interested in cosmology. Doubtless this very lack of vivid interest in such subjects helped to make him uncritical, and left him open to Pythagorean and other influences to which Aristotle, for example, was almost immune.

*4. Relations of Metaphysics and Ethics in the "Philebus."* Of all the dialogues, the *Philebus* perhaps goes farthest in the direction of Plato's ideal of a correlation of the various branches of knowledge.[16] The argument rests upon the fact that Socrates divides all things into four classes— (1) the finite, (2) the infinite, (3) a mixture of the two, resulting in the world as we have it,[17] and (4) the world-soul, or cause of the mixture.[18]

---

[1] *Timæus*, 35 A.  [2] *Ibid.*, 36 D, E.  [3] *Cf.* Gomperz, *op. cit.*, vol. III, p. 207.
[4] *Timæus*, 39 E.  [5] *Ibid.*, 40 A.  [6] *Ibid.*, 40 B.  [7] *Ibid.*, 44 D.
[8] *Ibid.*, 69 D–70 E.  [9] *Ibid.*, 81 A-B.  [10] *Ibid.*, 88 D, E, 90 D; *cf. Republic*, 588 A.
[11] *Cf. Phædrus*, 247 C.  [12] *Cf. Symposium*, 189 D, E.
[13] *Statesman*, 269 C, ff., esp. 274 A.  [14] *Laws*, 897 C.  [15] *Ibid.*, 898 E.
[16] *Republic*, 531 C, D, *Laws* 967 D, E.  [17] *Philebus*, 23 C, D; 26.
[18] *Ibid.*, 30, A, B.

Socrates's argument for the world-soul is similar to that related by Xenophon; our bodies are made up of the four elements; the cosmos is made up of the four elements, and may be considered to be a body; our bodies have souls; the larger mixture of the elements in the cosmos must have a soul also.[1] The good life consists, too, in a mixture [2] of finite and infinite,[3] or wisdom and pleasure,[4] in a harmony which realizes the good in man and in the All.[5]

5. *Comparison of Plato and Aristotle.* Thus Plato's works made use of a number of microcosmic arguments, without employing any definite term for them. It can almost be said that Aristotle employed the term, but not the arguments. There are only a few passages which suggest such views. Like Plato, Aristotle compared the state to an individual organism;[6] but the comparisons have behind them no concrete conception, sustained as in the *Republic*. Their background is rather that of the *Metaphysics*, or the *Ethics*, an abstract system for which they serve as illustrations; and while of course such a system of universally applicable principles exhibits the parts of the world as similar to one another, the system is so abstract and so general that microcosmic structures do not stand out with any prominence. Like Plato, again, Aristotle ascribes life, and action like that of plants and animals, to stars.[7] He thinks that the interior of the earth grows and decays like the body of a plant or animal;[8] he even ascribes "a kind of life," with generation and decay, to air and water in motion.[9] The planets do not move themselves;[10] they have each an "unmoved mover," sometimes, according to Erdmann,[11] called a soul. But the *De cœlo* is not as picturesque as the *Timæus* and does not invite the elaboration of its comparisons at the hands of a later age in the same way.[12]

---

[1] *Philebus*, 29–30.        [2] *Ibid.*, 61 B.        [3] *Ibid.*, 32 A, B.        [4] *Ibid.*, 60.
[5] *Ibid.*, 63 E.

[6] *Politics*, I, 5, 1254 a 28; III, 4, 1277 a 5; IV, 4, 1290 b 23; V, 3, 1302 b 34; V, 9, 1309 b 23; VI, 6, 1320 b 33; VII, 3, 1325 b 23. *Nic. Eth.*, VII, 10, 1152 a 20; IX, 8, 1168 b 31.

[7] *De cœlo*, II, 12, 292 a, b.        [8] *Meteorol.*, I, 14, 351.
[9] *De gen. an.*, IV, 10, 778 a.        [10] *De cœlo*, II, 8, 290 a.

[11] *History of Philosophy*, Eng. transl. Hough (London, 1891), vol. I, p. 157.

[12] Dieterici (*op. cit.*, I, 163), citing Zeller (*cf. Aristotle and the Earlier Peripatetics*, Eng. transl. Costelloe and Muirhead [London, 1897], vol. II, pp. 24–28), thinks that microcosmic theories begin to be grounded scientifically in *Hist. an.*, VIII, 1, 588 b 4, in Aristotle's teaching concerning the gradual transitions between the species, and the analogies (homologies) between them. Many later versions of the theory centered round the fact that, as Aristotle says, man has in him at their best qualities which the

*6. First Authentic Occurrence of the Term "Microcosm."* In spite of the fact that Aristotle does not make much use of such arguments, it is in his writings that the expression which afterward become the term "microcosm" is used, so far as we know, for the first time. In the *Physics*, Book VIII, chapter II, he considers objections to his theory of the eternity of motion; among them is the objection that animate beings seem to rouse themselves from a state of repose. He says:

"If this can happen in the living being, what hinders it from happening also in the All?—for if it happens in the little world (it happens) also in the great, [εἰ γὰρ ἐν μικρῷ κόσμῳ γίνεται, καὶ ἐν μεγάλῳ,] and if in the world, also in the Infinite, if it is possible for the Infinite to move itself." [1]

His answer is that there are hidden motions, both in things inanimate and in animals, which the objections fail to take into account. The character of the above passage, together with the fact that Aristotle does not use the term again throughout all his writings, leads one to suppose that he is here quoting the term from some opponent. For himself, he was too empirical in his biology and too abstract in his cosmogony to care for such a view. [2]

### 3. THE TEACHINGS OF THE STOICS

*1. Criticism of View of Some Investigators in this Field.* It has been maintained by several writers that microcosmic theories were prominent among the Stoics; [3] the implication usually is that the Stoics were agreed among themselves, and were explicit and systematic in their use of the theories. The chief support of this view is found in the work of Stein, [4] who thinks that the Stoic psychology, with its metaphysical and cosmological affiliations, afforded a broad and firm foundation upon which to

lower animals manifest less completely. But in these cases, as in his comparison of male and female with motion and matter (*De gen. an.*, II, 1, 731 b 24), or with form and matter (*Metaph.*, I, 6, 988 a 5) and in his view that the sense organs correspond to the four elements (*De sensu et sensili*, II, 437 a, 438 b), Aristotle's interests are quite remote from microcosmic theories. This is the case also in *De anima*, III, 8, 431 a, when he says that "in a manner the soul is the things which are."

[1] *Phys.*, VIII, 2, 252 b.

[2] Windelband is inaccurate when he says (*op. cit.*, p. 187) that the Stoics took the theory of man as a microcosm from Aristotle; even if the passage in Aristotle is meant to reflect his own views, it concerns animated beings in general rather than man.

[3] Windelband, *Hist. of Phil.*, pp. 14, n., 187; Bouché-Leclercq, *L'astrologie grecque*, p. 78; Arnold, *Rom. Stoicism*, p. 240; R. D. Hicks, *Stoic and Epicurean* (N. Y., 1910), p. 30.           [4] *Psych. der Stoa*, I, 206 ff.

work out a comparison between the universe and man, and that the whole rested within the general setting of Stoic pantheism.[1]  But the method which Stein uses to support these views is open to criticism.  He finds, among the fragments from the writings of the older Stoics, various passages about the world and, again, about man; a number of these he sets in parallel, showing that the two series exhibit a number of resemblances in the processes which they describe; and these he calls the Stoic teachings about macrocosm and microcosm.  But the method disregards temporal, geographical and individual differences.  In a case where writings are preserved only in scattered and fragmentary form, it is permissible, as we held in the case of the Pre-Platonic writings, to attempt to reconstruct a background, or to compare the fragments one with another; but either method alone, and the combination of both, must always be used with reserve, particularly when the fragments come from different authors.

2. *The Interests of the Stoics.*    Judging from their product as we find it, one would say that the interests of the Stoics were predominantly moral and religious.  As befitted philosophers, they discussed astronomy, physics and biology, and some of them had a more or less evident interest in logic and psychology; but, either because they wrote more ethical works, or else because their ethical writings seemed better worth preserving, we see them chiefly as moralists whose teachings verge upon those of a religion.[2]  If this estimate of them is accurate, we might expect to find them sometimes content with statements less precise than a closer study of the universe would have suggested.   Their interests were so predominantly ethical that their work differed from more exact sciences; and on the other hand their religion did not impose upon the individual writers the conformity required by a cult.  Accordingly we should expect to find not merely a certain looseness of statement, but also differences of opinion between the various men.

3. *Stoic Theories, according to the Fragments.*   It cannot be denied that the Stoic fragments show marked agreements between some of the writers, and doubtless more agreements than can be explained by the selecting or emendating operations of the doxographers.  Most of the Stoics probably agreed that the world was an animate and rational being; it is asserted of Zeno,[3] Chrysippus,[4] Apollodorus and Posidonius,[5] and

---

[1] *Psych. der Stoa*, pp. 206, 208, 214.          [2] Arnold, *Roman Stoicism*, p. 17.

[3] For several references, see J. von Arnim, *Stoicorum veterum fragmenta* (Leipzig, 1905) vol. I—Zeno, frgts. 110–114.

[4] *Ibid.*, vol. II, Chrysippus, frgts. 633–645.          [5] Diog. Laert. VII, lxx, 143.

indirectly of Cleanthes; [1] apparently only Boëthus of Sidon denied that the world was animate.[2]   Diogenes Laertius says that Zeno, Cleanthes, Chrysippus and Posidonius all taught that the world was subject to generation and corruption;[3] Stobæus has a passage asserting that Zeno, Cleanthes, and Chrysippus thought that the world would be reduced by fire to its primeval germinal state, from which it would at length arise again—an estimate of the Stoic teachings which was widespread in antiquity.[4] It is quite likely that these men agreed, again, that on general principles the human body and the universe must each have its ἡγεμονικόν, or guiding principle; [5] but they differed when it came to a question of locating this principle, both in the body and in the universe. With regard to the body, Zeno thought, according to Plutarch, that the guiding principle was in the head, [6] Chrysippus was said by others to have located it in the breast,[7] or heart.[8]   With regard to the universe, Cleanthes thought that the guiding principle was the sun; [9] Chrysippus said once that it was the sky, and, again, the æther.[10]   In general, once more, the Stoics held pantheistic views; but they differed in details here also.   Zeno is variously reported as having called the whole universe God, in agreement with Chrysippus,[11] and, again, as having called the æther God; [12] Cleanthes, according to Cicero, had no less than seven different views;[13] Diogenes of Babylonia said that God penetrates the universe as man's soul penetrates his body;[14] Posidonius said practically the same.[15]   It is evident that the presence in the Stoic fragments both of such agreements and such differences—and the list of either might be lengthened—must affect our estimate of the Stoic position with regard to microcosmic theories.   On the one hand, the agreements show that such theories were, if nothing more, at least implicit in the views of the Greek Stoics.   The fact, for

---

[1] *Cf.* Cicero, *De natura deorum*, I, xiv, 37; II, ix, 24.

[2] v. Arnim, *op. cit.*, vol. III, Boëthus, frgt. 6.

[3] *Op. cit.*, VII, lxx, 142.

[4] Stob., *Ecloga*, in v. Arnim, *op. cit.*, vol. II, frgt. 596.   Also 597–632.

[5] Plutarch, *Epitome*, IV, 21, in Diels, *Doxographi græci* (Berlin, 1879), p. 410.   *Cf.* Cicero, *De nat. deor.*, II, xi, 29.

[6] Plut., *Epit.*, in Diels, p. 411.

[7] Philodemus, *De pieta*, 16, in Diels, p. 549.

[8] Diog. Laert., VII, lxxxvi, 159; this may refer to other Stoics; v. Arnim prints it with those from Chrysippus (*op. cit.*, vol. II, frgt. 837).

[9] Diog. Laert., VII, lxx, 139.        [10] *Ibid., l. c.*        [11] *Ibid.*, VII, lxxii, 148.

[12] Cicero, *De nat. deor*, I, xiv, 36.        [13] *Ibid.*, I, xiv, 37.

[14] Philodem., *De piet.*, 15, in Diels, *Doxog.*, pp. 548–549.

[15] Diog. Laert., VII, lxx, 138.

example, that the universe was so generally regarded as animate left the way open for anyone interested in describing it further to express views of its origin and processes which would of course resemble the views held concerning embryology and physiology.[1] Similarly, the fact that it was regarded as rational led to psychological comparisons. But unless the comparison is made explicitly, or unless the fragments on which it is based come from the same author, one should not jump to the conclusion that the Stoics developed the theory of man as a microcosm.

Sometimes, indeed, the comparison does lie very near the surface—as when Zeno is said to have taught that, just as in the cosmos, man's "guiding principle" was in his head, which is of spherical form;[2] or as when Posidonius is cited to the effect that the $\nu o \hat{v} s$ of the cosmos enters as $\xi\iota s$ into our bones and sinews, and as $\nu o \hat{v} s$ into the guiding principle;[3] or as when, again, he is said to have ascribed $\pi \acute{a} \theta \eta$ to the earth.[4] Among the Roman Stoics, Seneca put the matter most clearly when he said

"The whole art of nature is imitation. . . . The place which God has in the world, the soul has in man; that which in the former is matter, is in us body."[5]

In his *Quæstiones naturales* he speaks of it as his own view that nature has organized the earth somewhat after the pattern of our bodies,[6] so that veins may be compared to water courses, arteries to air passages,[7] various fluids of the body to geological substances,[8] and injuries of the body to earthquakes.[9] Again, in connection with the doctrine of a world-conflagration, he says that whether the world is soul or body, everything that is to happen in it is bound up in its primordial condition, as is the case with the human embryo.[10] Of course Seneca may have taken such views from older Stoic sources; but it is obvious that in the present state of the sources we have in Seneca's explicit and consistent comparisons

---

[1] For some of these views, see Stein, *op. cit.*, vol. I, pp. 209 ff.

[2] Plut., *Epit.*, IV, 21, in Diels, *Doxog.*, p. 411. The word κόσμῳ is an emendation.

[3] Diog. Laert., VII, lxx, 138–139.

[4] Stob., *Ecl.*, in Diels, *Doxog.*, p. 383.

[5] *Epist.*, 65, 24. Stein (*op. cit.*, I, 208) says that this brief formulation of the theory is also found in Cornutus. Cicero in the "Dream of Scipio" makes Africanus argue for the divinity of the individual soul, which controls the body, just as God is the ruler of the world (*De republica*, VI, viii, 2). It is in connection with this passage that Macrobius, about 400 A. D., says that certain philosophers called the world a large man and man a short (-lived?) world (physici mundum magnum hominem et hominem brevem mundum esse dixerunt—*Comment. in Somn. Scip.*, II, xii, 11).

[6] *Quæst. nat.*, III, xv, 2.    [7] *Ibid.*, III, xv, 3, 5; VI, xiv, 2.    [8] *Ibid.*, III, xv, 4.

[9] *Ibid.*, VI, xxiv, 1–4.             [10] *Ibid.*, III, xxix, 2.

evidence for microcosmic theories more trustworthy than that afforded by the Greek fragments. Marcus Aurelius argued for the existence of a universal order from the fact that in man there is "a kind of world"; [1] this passage may also have reference to older sources. Whatever those sources may have contained, in the way of definitely expressed microcosmic views, one can say that in the fragments the views are implicit; their general agreements are enough to show this. On the other hand, their many differences, and the untrustworthy character of many of the sources make it a pointless task to try to weave a few of the fragments into a consistent and unified microcosmic theory which can be used as a measure for estimating fragments that remain outstanding.[2] In a word, so far as the evidence goes, the Greek Stoics were in much the same position as Plato; microcosmic arguments were used, but the theories were not very definitely elaborated. The term "microcosm," so far as one can find, was unknown.

4. *Relation of Microcosmic Theories to Stoic Ethics and Religion*. There is, as we intimated, reason to suppose that considerations of things physical were for the Stoics subordinate to ethical and religious interests. According to Diogenes Laertius, Zeno was the first to teach that "the end is to live according to nature, which is to live according to virtue." [3] Cicero says that Chrysippus held that man was placed here

"to contemplate and imitate the world; in no wise perfect, he is a kind of particle of the perfect"; [4]

Arnold thinks that in this microcosmic conception Chrysippus found a foundation for ethics.[5] The pantheistic views of some of the Stoics have been indicated. A passage attributed to Zeno suggested to Cicero that

"the universe displays all impulses of will and all corresponding actions just like ourselves when we are stirred through the mind and the senses." [6]

The two views are blended in the hauntingly beautiful words of Marcus Aurelius:

"Whatever is satisfactory to thee, O World, is satisfactory also to me. Nothing is too early or too late for me which to thee is in season. Like fruit to me, O Nature, is all that thy seasons bring." [7]

---

[1] *De rebus suis*, IV, 27; *cf.* Gataker's note.
[2] *Cf.* Stein's procedure, vol. I, p. 211.      [3] Diog. Laert. VII, liii, 87.
[4] *De natura deorum*, II, xiv, 37.      [5] *Rom. Stoicism*, p. 240.
[6] *De nat. deor.*, II, xxii, 58; transl. Arnold, *op. cit.*, p. 240.
[7] *De rebus suis*, IV, xxiii. *Cf.* V, xxi.

This saying typifies the Stoic ethics of submission to the order of nature, and the Stoic religion of contentment in one's relations to a universe regarded as quasi-personal. Such ethical and religious views are closely related to microcosmic theories, but they do not depend upon them in any definite way. One could say perhaps that the Stoic pantheism was an attitude rather than a system, and that the Stoic ethics was not solid, but fluid. Microcosmic theories did not enter into them much; it is more accurate to say that in the Stoic writings microcosmic theories begin to crystallize out of them.

### 4. JEWISH PHILOSOPHY IN THE GRÆCO-ROMAN PERIOD

*1. The Beginnings of the "Sefer Yezirah."* Other influences besides Stoicism were making for more definite microcosmic views. Perhaps from the second century B. C. date the beginnings of the Jewish *Sefer Yezirah*, or "Book of Creation." [1] According to this work in its later form, there are ten principles in the world, corresponding to ten letters and ten numbers. The letters of the alphabet, in groups of 3, 7, and 12, are made to interpret the processes of nature, the seasons, and the human body. [2] The origin of both the universe and man from permutations and combinations of the mystic powers of the letters points in the direction of a microcosmic theory. [3] But more definite indications appeared in the great syncretism at Alexandria.

*2. Philo's Theories of Man as the "Brachycosm."* Typical of the period of syncretism was Philo. His great aim was to harmonize Greek philosophy and Hebrew religion, in such a way as to avoid anthropomorphic conceptions of God. [4] All Jewish conceptions of man go back to the view that God created man in his own image. [5] Philo had two ways of explaining away the apparent anthropomorphism, and both ways involved the use of microcosmic theories. The first was to use the argument that what God is to the universe, the soul is to man; the resemblance between God and man, then, applies to the soul, not to the body. [6] This view is amplified when it is said that both in the universe and in man the mind is

---

[1] *Jewish Encyc.*, XII, 602–603.

[2] L. Goldschmidt, *Sepher Jesirah* (Frankfurt, 1894), pp. 21, 24.

[3] Cf. *Jewish Encyc.*, XII, 603.

[4] C. Bigg, *The Christian Platonists of Alexandria* (Oxford, 1886), p. 7.

[5] *Gen.*, I, 26–27.

[6] *De mundi opificio*, XXIII, 69–71. Cf. *Legum allegoriarum*, I, xxix, 91–92; *De monarchia*, I, 1; *De Abrahamo*, XVI, 74; *Ibid.*, XLVI, 272; *De migratione Abrahami*, XXXIII, 184–186.

composed of two portions, a superior and an inferior; [1] and that both the Logos in the universe and the reason in man divide and distribute all things which are under them.[2] The second way of explaining the verse in Genesis is to say that God made man, not in his image, but "after his image"; the image thus becomes an intermediate portion of creation, a copy of that which antedated it and a model of that which followed. This intermediate portion, in strict parallelism with the human soul, which is regarded as the undivided substratum of the six faculties, is declared to be the sky, or heaven, the undivided substratum of the six planets.[3] To reasoning in us corresponds the sun in the world.[4] The introduction of the intermediate stage between God and man makes possible the development of views that not merely is man's soul connected with the Logos, but his body is also connected with the material world [5] in an epitomizing way. In the working out of these latter views there seem to be two tendencies. There is first a Greek strain, according to which the four elements are mingled in proportion, which proportion extends to the differences between small and large, and makes man, as some (ἔνιοι) have declared, equal to the whole world; and these men,

"going from one thing to another, have called man a little world, and the world a large man." [6]

In another work, an argument for the existence of God is made on the ground that if there were no providence and moving spirit in the universe there could be no motion, and the psychical processes of man, who is "made like a little world in the great world" would then be inexplicable.[7]

---

[1] *De vita Mosis*, III, xiii, 127.

[2] *Quis rerum divinarum hæres sit*, XLVIII, 234–236.

[3] *Quis rer. div. haer.*, XLVIII, 230–236.

[4] *Ibid.*, LIII, 263–264; cf. *De posteritate Caini*, XVI, 55–58.

[5] *De mund. opif.*, LI, 146.

[6] *Quis rer. div. haer*, XXIX–XXXI, 146–156. Βραχὺν μὲν κόσμον τὸν ἄνθρωπον, μέγαν δ᾽ ἄνθρωπον ἔφασαν τὸν κόσμον εἶναι. The words are remarkably like those of Macrobius, quoted in a note on the preceding paragraph, and seem to point to lost sources for explicit microcosmic theories. Perhaps the use of βραχύν may contain a trace of temporal comparison between the universe and man (cf. *New Engl. Dict.*, art. "Macrocosm," and the suggested translation of Macrobius, above). Philo called the world "the largest man" in *De migr. Abr.*, XXXIX, 220. Cf. *De Abr.*, XV–XVI, 72–74. Neumark (*Gesch. der jud. Phil. . . .* , vol. II, p. 405) thinks that the *Quis rer. div. hær.*, especially in view of its treatment of man as the microcosm, may have been intended by Philo as a somewhat systematic and comprehensive statement of his philosophy.

[7] *De providentia*, I, 40. "tamquam parvus mundus in magno mundo factus est." See C. Richter's edition of Philo's works (Leipzig, 1828–30), vol. VIII, p. 24, n.

Again, we find the view that man is at once every kind of animal—terrestrial, aquatic, flying, and, thanks to his visual perception of distance, celestial.[1]  Besides these views, which exhibit more or less definite traces of Greek influence, there is another strain which Philo himself attributes to the " Chaldeans." He declares that just as Abraham left Chaldea, so his readers should leave the speculations of the Chaldeans, and particularly their notions of God; still he thinks it is allowable to accept the doctrine of a sympathy existing between the parts of the universe.[2]  Thus the sky, or heaven, the intermediate "image" between God and man, was the beginning of creation, and man was the end, and they belong together in a unified whole.  Man is

> "if one must speak the truth, a little sky [or, heaven], bearing within him as images many natures star-formed, in his arts and sciences and . . . speculations." [3]

In a passage which may be either Greek or oriental it is said that in the creation the number 7 attained importance in heaven and, in accordance with a certain natural sympathy, was extended also to men, where its importance is pointed out in the seven divisions of the soul and of the body, the seven motions, secretions, vowels, and notes of the musical scale.[4]  Another passage which is hardly Greek and hardly Jewish in its affiliations is that with the elaborate description of the High Priest's vestments, which constitute an imitation of the universe; the High Priest is bidden

> "if he can not be worthy of the Creator, to strive constantly to be worthy of that world whose image he bears, . . . be changed from the nature of a man in a way into the nature of the world, and if it is right to say—and it *is* right, not to be false in speaking about what is the truth—to be a little world." [5]

Microcosmic theories were also pressed into service to help Philo's curious interpretations of the Scriptures by the allegorical method.  Thus, three cities of Egypt are taken as symbols of faculties of the soul,[6] and

---

[1] *De mund. opif.*, LI, 146; perhaps suggested by Aristotle, *De hist. an.*, VIII, 1, 588 b.

[2] *De migr. Abr.*, XXXII, 176–183.  On the Babylonian origin or affiliations of microcosmic theories, see works of Berthelot, Cumont and v. Lippmann, cited in the Introduction, above.

[3] *De mund. opif.*, XXVII, 82: βραχύν, εἰ δεῖ ταληθὲς εἰπεῖν, οὐρανόν . . .

[4] *Ibid.*, XXXV–XLIII, 104–128.

[5] *De vit. Mos.*, II (III), xiv, 133–135: καὶ εἰ θέμις εἰπεῖν—θέμις δ' ἀψευδεῖν περὶ ἀληθείας λέγοντα—βραχὺς κόσμος εἶναι.

[6] *De poster. Caini*, XVI, 55–58.

the verse, "He that planted the ear, shall he not hear?" [1] is cited as support of the view that the senses in man are to be compared to trees; [2] and in both these passages, man is called the βραχὺς κόσμος. It is this repeated use of a term for the theory, and of this term in particular, some-times with his curious half-apologetic phrase about speaking the truth in the matter, that constitutes the chief difference between Philo and those who preceded him, so far as their works are known to us. Its use means that the theory of such a relation between the universe and man is no longer merely implicit in philosophy, but is beginning to be com-monly recognized. In general, it may be said that in the works of Philo the chief function of the theory was to help to harmonize the Hebrew and the Greek views of the world and of man. And linked in, as it were, between these two great bodies of thought, microcosmic theories re-mained in Jewish philosophy for centuries. [3]

## 5. Neo-Pythagoreans and Eclectics

*1. The Persistence of Pythagoreanism.* The sequences of history are often traceable to the writing rather than to the living of it. It is not quite accurate to speak of a revival of Pythagoreanism; for one must not suppose that in a world so easily capable of being fascinated as was that of the Græco-Roman period, Pythagoreanism ever died out. If it did, either the Greek mystery religions or the Babylonian number specula-tions or Egyptian magical formulæ slipped imperceptibly into its place. But as time went on Pythagoreanism, like the other philosophies of the period, began to develop more definite microcosmic theories. It is im-possible to fix the dates of the writings, but it may be taken for granted that they do not belong to the periods of the men whose names they bear. Thus the view ascribed to Pythagoras, [4] that man is a microcosm because he has in him the four elements, and all the powers of the cosmos as they are found in plants and animals, and, crowning the whole, the divine power of reason, is more like the Alexandrian than the Athenian way of stating the theory. Of the other pseudonymous works, the *De anima mundi et natura* of the so-called Timæus Locrius emphasizes the rôle of

[1] *Ps. XCIV*, 9.

[2] *De plantatione Noë*, VII, 28.

[3] References to traces of the theory in the Talmud in K. Pollak, *Abot d. R. Natan.* (Frankfurt, 1905), pp. 109-110; in the Midrashim, in B. Beer's article (p. 160; cited in Introduction, above).

[4] Photius, *Bibliothecon*, codex 249 (ed. Bekker, II, 440-a).

numbers, proportions, harmonies,[1] and the presence of the four element
in the human fœtus,[2] and says that a process similar to breathing goes on
in inorganic things.[3]   In a work called *De universi natura*, which comes to
us under the name of Ocellus Lucanus, it is said that man is a part of a
household, and of a city, "and this, which is the greatest thing, of the
world." [4]   In a fragment of another work there is the view that life holds
the body together, and the cause of this is the soul; harmony holds the
world together, and the cause of this is God; peace holds families and
states together, and the cause of it is the law.[5]   Another application of an
argument from analogy to a social problem is found in what remains of a
work of Sthenidas, who believed that the world and its parts are alive,
that the peace of a city ought to imitate the concord of the world, and
that the relation of a king to his subjects is like that of God to the world.

  *2. Eclectics: Reference of Galen to Possible Lost Sources.*   The ancient
eclectics were in a more favorable position for the study of sources of the
microcosmic theories than later generations have been.   In the case of
Galen, who may be grouped with the eclectics, although he was notable
on his own account, there is one passage which, taken together with those
of Philo and Macrobius, and even David of Nerken, noted above, again
strengthens the probability that some more ancient writers, perhaps Pre-
Platonic, spoke definitely about microcosms.   In this passage, which
occurs in a teleological argument, Galen says that men of old time, who
were proficient in the study of nature, said that a living being was a kind
of little world.[8]

## 6. THE NEO-PLATONISTS

  *1. The Place of Microcosmic Theories in the "Enneads" of Plotinus.*   The
fairest product of the great syncretism at Alexandria was Neo-Platonism.
For Plotinus, the terms of any possible comparison between the universe
and man were likely to be lost in the metaphysical unity of the First

---

[1] F. Mullach, *Fragmenta philosophorum græcorum* (Paris, 1881), vol. II, p. 34,
section 3.

[2] *Ibid.*, p. 41, sec. 5.          [3] *Ibid.*, p. 42; sec. 7.

[4] Mullach, *op. cit.*, vol. I, p. 402; IV, 3.   Eng. transl. by T. Taylor (London, 1831).
By a slight emendation of τὸ μέγιστον κόσμου to read τοῦ μεγίστου κόσμου, this passage could be relieved of a rather awkward construction, and be made to refer to
the microcosmic theory.

[5] Mullach, I, p. 407.          [6] *Ibid.*, p. 536.          [7] *Ibid.*, pp. 537–8.

[8] *De usu partium*, III, x, 241. Τὸ ζῷον οἷον μικρόν τινα κόσμον εἶναί φασιν
ἄνδρες παλαιοὶ περὶ φύσιν ἱκανοί.

Being, or dissolved in his mystical absorption in the Highest. But, whatever might be the ultimate truth, the doctrine of emanations implied that there were certain more or less transitory resemblances between these stages of the world process. The resemblance is such that the cosmos may fairly be called an image, always moulding itself.[1] In the case of a living being, under a single ἀρχή, one can learn of one part from another; and the comparison is suggested between our members as parts of our bodies, and us as parts of the world.[2] The parts of the universe may be regarded even as wholes.[3] Just as the parts of a living body contribute to its life, and just as man is moved by animated powers within him, so the things contained in the universe, each living its own life, make up the life of the whole.[4] The universe is a single living being,[5] but lives differently in each of its parts.[6] Sometimes, as in the body, the parts are antagonistic one to another.[7] The resemblances between the universe and living beings are not merely biological, or physiological; they are also psychological. The world has no external objects nor organs of sensation, but has what might now be called a kind of proprioceptive system—for, says Plotinus, just as we apprehend one part by means of another, what hinders the All from seeing the planetary region by means of that region which is fixed, and from seeing the earth and what is contained in it by means of the planetary region?[8] Although it is declared that the world-soul differs from ours in some respects,[9] the parallelism of world-soul and individual soul is repeatedly employed. The world-soul directs the All according to reason, like the ἀρχή in each living being, from which each of the parts of the living being is fashioned, and by which they are coördinated with the whole, of which they are parts.[10] Both the world-soul and the individual soul are represented as divided into higher and lower parts.[11] Again, it is said that to the three principles from which the world has been produced—the One, the Intelligence, and the world-soul—must correspond three principles in us.[12] Of our soul, one portion remains in the highest region, another descends to the world of mundane affairs, and a third remains in an intermediate

---

[1] *Enneads*, II, iii, 17, 148 C.   (Creuzer's text.)        [2] II, iii, 7, 141 A.

[3] II, iii, 7, 141 C.

[4] IV, iv, 36, 431 C; *cf.* IV, iv, 45, 439 A.        [5] IV, iv. 35, 429 B.

[6] IV, iv, 36, 431 A, B.        [7] IV, iv, 32, 426 D.

[8] IV, iv, 24, 417 B, C.        [9] II, ix, 7, 205 B.

[10] II, iii, 13, 143 F; *cf.* III, i, 2, 229 D, E; IV, iii, 7, 376, E, F; III, i, 8, 233 F, G; III, v, 3, 294, C, D.

[11] IV, iii, 4, 375 A, B; *cf.* II, iii, 9, 142 D, E.        [12] V, i, 10, 491 A–E.

region.[1] Once more, the rank of some living beings in the universe is compared to that of the second power of the soul and the lowest parts of the soul in man,[2] respectively.

In this general setting of physiological and psychological analogies between the universe and living beings, Plotinus gives expression to one or two views which are quite definitely microcosmic. In one passage of the *Enneads* one is reminded of the opinion which as we saw was ascribed by Galen to certain men of antiquity, and which was alluded to by Aristotle—Plotinus says that just as the world-soul elaborates the cosmos, so "the reasons in the seeds fashion and form the living beings [or, animals], as, in a way, little worlds." [3] In another passage, Plotinus has a phrase which marks the point at which a new application of the microcosmic theory begins to emerge. Aristotle, in reflecting upon the fact that we have experience of the world, had said that the soul is, in a way, the things that are, and that knowledge and sensation are subdivided (into potential and actual) to correspond to the things.[4] Plotinus has a view which is in itself similar, but which, placed in the Neo-Platonic setting, appears in a different aspect. He says that our soul has an intermediate position between things superior and things inferior; that the soul "is many things, or rather, all things"; [5] and, he adds, "We are each an intelligible world." [6] Thus the way was opened for what may be called epistemological microcosmic theories. And when he says in another passage that we should so arrange that the ἀρχαί within us shall be both ends and wholes, and this according to the best in our nature,[7] the way is almost open for a microcosmic theory in ethics. In one or two less important and more fantastic ways, also, Plotinus suggests some of the theories that developed later. More than Plato, he emphasizes the parallelism between living beings and the earth. Since so many living beings are seen to arise from it, why not, he asks, say that it is a living being? [8] He thinks it is not absurd to suppose that the earth has a soul.[9] It is not necessary that the earth's organs should be like ours; even among the living beings on the earth all organs are not the same.[10] The earth is sensitive to great things, not small, and can hear and nod assent

---

[1] II, ix, 2, 201 A, B.        [2] II, iii, 13, 144 C, D.
[3] IV, iii, 10, 379–380. τὰ ζῶα οἶον μικρούς τινας κόσμους.
[4] *De anima*, III, 8, 431 b.        [5] *Enneads*, III, ɪv, 3, 285 A, 284 G.
[6] *Ibid.*, 284 G. καὶ ἔσμεν ἕκαστος κόσμος νοητός . . .
[7] III, ix, 2, 357 C.        [8] IV, iv, 22, 414 C.        [9] IV, iv, 26, 419 B.
[10] IV, iv, 26, 419 (1) A.

to prayers, although not in the way we would do.[1]  Finally, Plotinus
verges upon astrology in his use of the doctrine of sympathy.  The parts
of the universe are sympathetic, like the parts of a living being.[2]  All
things are coördinated, and there are analogies which make divinations
possible.[3]  Souls in their ascents and descents conform to the universal
order, and there are signs of their fates in the positions of the stars.[4]
Altogether, microcosmic theories were more explicit in the new Platonism
than in the old.  Although, judged from his works, particularly in their
present arrangement, Plotinus himself was not very systematic, he was
consistent enough so that it was not difficult to construct philosophical
systems along the lines which he laid down.  His use of microcosmic
theories made these systems more concrete and definite than they might
otherwise have been.  As the vast influence of Plotinus widened, other
features of his teachings were more prominent; but the fact that his
mysticism was the consummation rather than the contradiction of the
processes observable in things concrete and definite accommodated microcosmic theories and carried them along with it.

2. *Traces of Microcosmic Theories among the Successors of Plotinus.*
The immediate successors of Plotinus reflect his views, with slight
changes and additions.  According to Stobæus, Porphyry called man
μικρὸν διάκοσμον.[5]  Jamblichus, by the introduction of triadic formulas
and elaborate speculations,[6] helped to crystallize the Neo-Platonic teachings, although they often crystallized in strange colors.  Chalcidius, in
his commentary on the *Timæus*, repeats the familiar doctrines that man
is formed from the elements which compose the world; that his soul is of
the same nature as the world-soul; and that he was called "mundum
brevem" by the ancients (veteribus).[7]  For Proclus, the first triad is
Being, ζωή, and νοῦς; and ζωή is a διάκοσμος, and gives rise to a new
triad.[8]  It is said of him that he placed his dialectic at the service of the
microcosmic theory;[9] he says that the division of the genera is like the
demiurgic division of the cosmos into factors which are related to one
another as contradictories.  The ideal city of Plato, if it is to be ordered

---

[1] IV, iv, 26, 418 (2) B, C.        [2] IV, iv, 32, 426 A, B; *cf.* IV, iv, 35, 429 B.
[3] III, iii, 6, 276 C, D, E; *cf.* II, iii, 5, 140 C; II, iii, 7, 141 A.
[4] IV, iii, 12, 381 E, F.        [5] Stob., *Florileg.*, XXI, 27.
[6] Erdmann, *Hist. of Phil.*, vol. I, p. 248.
[7] *Commentarius in Timæum Platonis* (in Mullach, *op. cit.*, vol. II), CC.  *Cf.*
CCXXX.
[8] Erdmann, *op. cit.*, vol. I, p. 251.
[9] Bouché-Leclercq, *L'astrologie grecque*, p. 77, n. 1.

after the model of the cosmos, ought to be divided into higher and lower
or heavenly and earthly portions. The polities of the good are like the
order of the heavens.[1] Proclus thought that in a theory of the world the
nature of man ought to be discussed completely—for man is a microcosm
and all the things which the world contains are, as was said in the *Philebus*
contained partially in him; he has a rational soul akin to the world-soul
and a terrestrial body derived from the four elements.[2] Again, various
mental and bodily functions were coördinated with divinities and heavenly bodies.[3] Hierocles of Alexandria taught that the nature of the visible
world is everywhere conformable to itself by analogy. The "upper
part" is enamelled with stars and filled with intelligent beings, while the
lower part has vegetables and animals endowed only with sense. Man
is intermediate, partaking of the nature of each.[4] Thus Neo-Platonism
offered a framework such as was used by some mediæval and also some
modern systems; and the microcosmic theories helped to make the
framework articulate and intelligible.

## 7. MYSTERY AND MAGIC IN GREEK AND GRÆCO-ROMAN PHILOSOPHY

*1. Mystery and Magic not Confined to the Period of Decline.* We have
noted in the case of the Neo-Pythagoreans that, along with the more
prominent movements in Greek philosophy, there persisted a strain of
speculations similar to those of Babylon and Egypt. It is impossible to
fix definite dates and origins for many of its documents; one gets the
impression that as the great thinkers pass into silence the lesser voices
are heard more frequently, but this is in part an illusion due to the arrangement of historical materials. Enough can be determined concerning dates and places to show that mystery and magic formed a kind of
background or undercurrent for the philosophy of the whole period.

*2. Topical Arrangement of these Writings.* The obscurity of most of
these writers will justify a topical rather than a biographical and chronological treatment. By grouping them in this way it is not meant to
imply that all held the same views or that similar words used by two or
more writers had the same implications. Such a grouping shows, in

[1] Proclus, *Commentarius in Platonis Timæum*, I, 11 C; I, 62 D.
[2] *Ibid.*, I, 2 B, C; *cf.* V, 292 A.     [3] V, 348 A.
[4] Hierocles, *Commentarius in Aurea Carmina* . . . ed. P. Needham (Cambridge,
1709), pp. 178–181. W. K. Clifford, in his *Lectures and Essays* (London, 1879; vol. II,
pp. 267–268), appears to have read into Hierocles a more definite microcosmic theory
than the sources warrant.

general, that microcosmic views pervaded not merely the great schools of philosophy, which we have considered, but also the obscure circles of the cults.

*3. Use of the Term " Microcosm" or its Equivalent.* Considering first the writers who are explicit in their use of the term " microcosm" or a similar expression, we find that they belong toward the close of the period, rather than in the pre-Alexandrian days. Thus Manilius (first century A. D.) says that man has a world in himself, and is the image of God.[1] Solinus (third century) calls man a "lesser world"—minorem mundum.[2] Firmicus Maternus (fourth century), who may have used the same source as Manilius, says that man, conformed to the nature of the world,[3] made in imitation of it,[4] and ruled by the same forces, is sustained by the sun, moon and stars as a kind of little world.[3] Microcosmic theories are found in several of the writings ascribed to Hermes Trismegistos, which may perhaps be dated during the third and following centuries.[5] In a formula of the "Emerald Table," important for this school, it is declared that "that which is beneath is like that which is above."[6] In the *Poimandres*, one of the principal works, appears a symbolic cosmic figure, "Man-Shepherd, Mind of All Masterhood,"[7] who acts as interpreter of the mysteries. It is declared that the world is the son of God, and man the son of the world,[8] or the "second world."[9] According to Berthelot, Olympiodorus (fifth century) says that Hermes Trismegistos says that man is a microcosm, possessing all the attributes of the great world.[10] In a hermetic work edited by Ideler, it is said that the wise men say that man is a world.[11] In the *Virgin of the World*, another hermetic work, there is the view that the earth lies in the midst of the cosmos with parts of the earth-body oriented with reference to the cosmos.

[1] Manilius, *Astronomica*, IV, 888 ff.

[2] Quoted by Lobeck, II, 921.

[3] Firmicus Maternus, *Matheseos Libri VIII*, book III, pref.

[4] *Ibid.*, III, 1, 15; *cf.* III, 1, 10 and 16.

[5] *Encyc. Brit.* (11th ed.), vol. XIII, art. "Hermes Trismegistus."

[6] *The Hermetic Museum*, Eng. transl. Waite (London, 1893) vol. II, pp. 320–321. *Cf.* E. Underhill, *Mysticism*, p. 191.

[7] *Thrice Greatest Hermes*, Eng. transl. Mead (London, 1906), vol. II, p. 3.

[8] Quoted by J. Kroll, *Die Lehre des Hermes Trismeg.*, p. 233.

[9] Quoted by Bouché-Leclercq, *L'astrol. grecque*, p. 77, n. 1.

[10] Berthelot, cited by v. Lippmann, *Entstehung und Ausbreitung der Alchemie*, p. 101.

[11] J. Ideler, *Physici et medici grœci minores* (Berlin, 1841), vol. I, p. 387. A microcosmic theory is also found in the work of an anonymous writer, printed in vol. I, p. 303.

In the midst of the earth is the sacred place (of the cult) just as the heart, the seat of the soul, is in the central part of the body—and for this reason, that man should not only have all other things, but be in addition intelligent and wise, as if he were born and sustained in the heart (of things).[1]

*4. Relations between Parts of the Human Body and Gods, or Parts of the Universe.* Along with the general theory to the effect that man is a microcosm should be mentioned the more fragmentary related views that various separate parts of the human body, traits of human character, or periods of human life correspond to the position or function of various gods or various portions of the universe. These include the Orphic view that sky, stars, water, sun, etc., make up the parts of the body of Zeus, who is at once ruler of the world and the world itself.[2] Views somewhat similar are found in Varro[3] and Plutarch.[4] According to many writers, the universe has a right and a left side.[5] Among those who assert a correspondence between parts of the human body and various planets or divinities are Melampus (third century B. C.), who thus assigns the fingers.[6] Fulgentius (fifth century A. D.) ascribes to Democritus such a distribution of the various parts of the body.[7] One of the hermetic writings assigns parts of the body to regions of the Zodiac,[8] as does Manilius;[9] this very old view persisted for centuries. Among those who assert on their own account, or report others as asserting that human characteristics and qualities are in correspondence with certain stars or divinities are Macrobius and Servius, in their commentaries on Cicero and Vergil, respectively;[10] the view is also found in the *Poimandres*.[11] Vitruvius (first century, B. C.) compared the symmetry of the human body not only to the universe, but also to a temple.[12] The view that the different periods of man's life were in relations to planets or divinities was widespread in the period of Græco-Roman decline.[13]

*5. Relations of Parts of the Universe Other than Man.* Again it is

---

[1] Stob., *Eclog.*, I, 41–45, 990–992. *Cf.* Kroll, *op. cit.*, p. 159.

[2] Quoted by Lobeck, *op. cit.*, II, 912. *Cf.* E. B. Tylor, *Primitive Culture* (London, 1913), vol. I, p. 350.

[3] Quoted by Lobeck, II, 920.       [4] *Ibid.*, II, 914.

[5] For references, see Lobeck, II, 915–920.

[6] *Ibid.*, II, 927.       [7] *Ibid.*, II, 926. *Cf.* the view of Servius.

[8] Ideler, *op. cit.*, I, 387; Lobeck, *op. cit.*, II, 926.

[9] Bouché-Leclercq, *op. cit.*, p. 319.       [10] Lobeck, II, 932–933.

[11] *Ibid.*, 934.       [12] *Architectura*, III, I, 10, 15.

[13] v. Lippmann, *op. cit.*, p. 219. *Cf.* Lobeck, II, 937–938.

declared that portions of the universe, quite apart from man, are related
to one another in significant ways. Thus, according to Quintilian (first
century A. D.) each season of the year resembles an element, and each
corresponds to a number.[1] And very widespread was the Pythagorean
doctrine that the universe had some significant connection with the
strings of a lyre, although there were curious variations about the number
of strings concerned.[2]

   6. *Relation of Microcosmic Theories to Astrology.*  All these supposed
correspondences between the universe and man either grew out of, or
naturally led to astrology, and various forms of divination.   Such
practices were doubtless in some cases elements in situations which the
microcosmic theories attempted to rationalize; in other cases they were
possibly grotesque attempts to turn the microcosmic theories to practical
use.  According to Bouché-Leclercq, the theory of man as the microcosm
helped in the astrological formulations of birth-lore.[3]  The earth was
divided into regions belonging to the various planets, to the signs of the
Zodiac (*i. e.*, the region of the fixed stars), or to both.  The division could
apply to categories of things or to living creatures.  And since man was
thought of as a microcosm, the division made of the world could be
repeated in him, and be evident in a distribution of astral influences
among his bodily organs and psychic powers.  As compared with the
planets, the Zodiacal regions had the advantage of being fixed and of
offering a larger number of divisions; hence the latter, with the fixed
stars, were looked upon as responsible for permanent forms and relations,
while the planets were held to influence individual and changeable things.
And the method was reversible—for the physiology of the human microcosm, as it came to be more and more studied, made possible an abridgment of astrology, making that rambling pseudo-science a little more
definite and compact.[4]

## 8. SUMMARY: MICROCOSMIC THEORIES IN ANCIENT PHILOSOPHY

Theories that portions of the universe which vary in size imitate one
another in structures and processes, and particularly, the theory that
man is a microcosm, or little world, are implicit in the fragments of
some of the most important of the Greek philosophers prior to Plato, and
there is a probability that some of them expressed such views more

[1] Lobeck, II, 945.      [2] *Ibid.*, II, 941–947.
[3] Bouché-Leclercq, *op. cit.*, p. 83.      [4] *Ibid.*, pp. 311–318.

definitely in writings that are now lost. Such theories remain implicit in the more systematic of Plato's dialogues, and, with the exception of a single passage, in the writings of Aristotle. So far as the evidence goes, we must say that even the Greek Stoics did not formulate such views in so many words although it is quite likely that they shared the views and may have expressed them in works no longer extant. The theory that man is a microcosm becomes clearly explicit in the writings of Philo, after the syncretism at Alexandria. Possibly the infusion of Babylonian or Egyptian elements here precipitated the theory in this explicit form. Microcosmic theories helped to render Neo-Platonism articulate. Throughout the Græco-Roman, and even the earlier Greek period, such views were closely allied with the lore of the mystery cults, magicians, and astrologers. In general, as the theories became more explicit, their effect and function in the uncritical ancient world was to furnish a framework for incipient philosophical systems and to concentrate attention upon man as a distinguished and favored member of the universe.

# CHAPTER II

# MICROCOSMIC THEORIES IN THEOLOGICAL TRADITIONS

## 1. CHARACTERISTICS OF THEOLOGICAL TRADITIONS

The phrase "theological traditions" is here used to describe the period in the history of philosophy usually referred to as mediæval. Neither designation is altogether suitable; but the general characteristics of the period from our point of view are a dominance of theological interest and a larger measure of conscious dependence upon the work of the past than is countenanced in what we know as the humanistic or the modern periods. It is easy to overestimate such conscious dependence, and the method it suggests must be used with caution. Allowance must be made in philosophy for individual creativeness; failure to do so would make every historian a Diogenes Laertius or a Hegel. But if ever a continuity of thinking and a sequence of influence is to be expected, it is within the ecclesiastical organizations where there is a certain uniformity of background and where, in the works allowed to survive, a virtue has been made of conformity to the faith that was in the men of old time. Under theological traditions are to be included not only those of the Christians, but also those of the Jewish and Arabian philosophers. At the risk of some distortion of historical perspective, we shall consider these three groups separately; this procedure appears to be the more justifiable in view of the fact that, as we shall try to show, the influence of the three traditions upon one another, so far as microcosmic theories are concerned, was not as great as has sometimes been supposed.

## 2. MICROCOSMIC THEORIES IN CHRISTIAN TRADITIONS

1. *Survivals of Greek Thought.* The microcosmic theories, as we have seen, had their roots in Greek thought, or in oriental strata which lay near it. They did not belong among the ideas specifically Christian; Christianity for the most part took over Hebraic ideas of the creation of the world and of man, and threw most of its emphasis upon the destiny of the world and upon man's salvation. In the writings of the Church Fathers microcosmic theories sometimes appear, but they are of minor

importance. Sometimes they occur along with other features evidently
absorbed from the Greeks; sometimes they are cited in order to be refuted;
sometimes they help to soften what otherwise stand out as harsh lines in
the Christian system; sometimes they provide almost a complete summary of the scientific views of these writers. But they never become
vital. They remain just enough in evidence so that the ideas do not quite
die out; one may say that they are latent or recessive throughout the
Christian mediæval period.

2. *Controversies of Orthodoxy with Heresy and Paganism.* One early
Christian writer in an effort to win the Greeks took over in so many
words the view that man is a microcosm; the fact is the more remarkable
when one notes that this is done by Clement of Alexandria in his *Horta-
tory Address*, a work in which he urges the abandonment of many Greek
conceptions. He says that the "new song" of Christianity has made the
universe a harmony, and has brought harmony especially to man who,
composed of body and soul, is a little universe.[1] For a century or two
following the time of Clement, the controversies with various Gnostic
sects seem to have driven the Church Fathers to oppose microcosmic
theories rather than adopt them. Thus the view of one Monoïmus, that
"man is the universe, the originating cause of all things," is combated by
Hippolytus;[2] and the speculation of the Basilidians, to the effect that
the "Abraxas," or Source of emanations, has produced 365 numbers,
corresponding to the number of days in the year, and the alleged number
of members of the human body, is attacked by Epiphanius.[3] The author
of the *Disputation of Archelaus with Manes* gives as the view of the latter
an account of creation which recalls that of the *Timæus*, and says that
Manes believes that all men have roots which are linked beneath with
those above, and that the body of man is called a cosmos in relation to
the great cosmos.[4] In the midst of his conflict with the paganism of
Africa, Arnobius denounces men who think of themselves too highly, and
refutes the argument that the soul is immortal and that man is a microcosm made and formed after the fashion of the universe, by pointing out

---

[1] *Cohort. ad Gentes*, I; Migne, *Patr. Gr.*, vol. I, col. 60.    Clement's expression is
"τὸν σμικρὸν κόσμον."

[2] *Refutatio omn. heres.* (ed. P. Wendland, Leipzig, 1916), VIII, xii, 2.

[3] *Adv. hæres.*, I, ii, 7; Migne, *Patr. Gr.*, vol. XLI, col. 316.

[4] *Disputatio*, 8; Migne, *Patr. Gr.*, vol. X, col. 1412. On the Manichæan belief, see
F. Legge, *Forerunners and Rivals of Christianity* (Cambridge, 1915), vol. II, pp. 307,
353ff.

that a man may be as senseless as a stone, and that it is only through God's goodness that any soul becomes immortal.[1]

*3. Microcosmic Theories as an Offset to Origen's Doctrine of the Body.* As Christianity became more firmly established the Fathers apparently had less dread of the microcosmic theories; some writers even found a use for them within the Christian system. According to Harnack, Origen's idea that the body was a prison of the soul was contrasted, during the period of the development of dogma, with the view that man was a microcosm, having received parts from the two created worlds, the higher and the lower. Harnack thinks that this conception was the only one which contained a coherent theory that formally could be considered of equal value with that of Origen; but he points out that it could, after all, remain only a theory, because in its implications it was out of harmony with the dominant theology.[2] From the time of Clement of Alexandria to that of Thomas Aquinas there are traces of microcosmic theories in patristic and scholastic literature; a score or more of writers repeat one or more of the Greek views, with only a few noteworthy modifications. In all these writings the theories impart a suggestion of naturalism to what would otherwise be almost unmodified supernaturalism; they direct the attention, for a moment, to the physical universe, and to man as a member of it.

*4. Summary of Greek Views as Repeated Without Essential Modifications.* Of course in their use of the microcosmic theories the Christian writers had views of the origin and destiny of the world and of man which differed from those of the Greeks; but they found it quite possible to place in this setting some Greek views of the relations of man and the universe. Most common was the view noted above, to the effect that in the soul and body of man two worlds were mingled. Gregory Nazianzen says that this makes man "a kind of second world, great in littleness." [3] Nemesius [4] and Cosmas Indicopleustis [5] emphasize the unifying function of man, who binds together the two worlds. Other statements to the effect that man combines the higher and the lower are found in the works

---

[1] *Adv. gentes*, II, 25; Migne, *Patr. Lat.*, vol. V, col. 851.

[2] *History of Dogma*, Eng. transl. Buchanan (Boston, 1903), vol. III, pp. 258–9.

[3] *De pasch.*, Orat. LXV, vii; Migne, *Patr. Gr.*, vol. XXXVI, col. 632.

[4] *De nat. hom.*, I, 14; Migne, *Patr. Gr.*, vol. XL, col. 512.

[5] *The Christian Topography of Cosmas . . .*, VII, 289, Eng. transl. McCrindle, (London, Hakluyt Society, 1897), pp. 284–285.

of Gregory the Great,[1] Maximus the Confessor,[2] John of Damascus,[3] Arnold of Bonneval,[4] Gundisallinus,[5] and Thomas Aquinas;[6] thus the view was incorporated into the two great doctrinal systems, in the East and West, as well as in less important works. The view that man shares the faculties and powers of all the lower species is also found in a number of writers. Gregory of Nyssa, indeed, thought the opinion that man is a little world, composed of the same elements as the universe, was unworthy of the majesty of man, since the lower forms of life are also made of those elements, and, according to the Church, the greatness of man consists in his being in the image of the nature of the Creator.[7] But a fourth century Christian liturgy of Alexandria calls man the κοσμοπολίτην, containing the κόσμου κόσμον;[8] and later writers combined the essentials of both views which Gregory of Nyssa had contrasted. Thus Maximus,[9] and after him Scotus Erigena, called man the "workshop of all things";[10] the latter added that all things were contained in man as smaller numbers are contained in a larger number.[11] John of Damascus says that man has a body composed of the four elements; shares with the plants the powers of nourishment, growth, and reproduction; shares with the animals the senses and locomotion; shares with incorporeal and intelligible natures his reason—hence man is a little world.[12] Such views were held by men as widely separated as Gregory the Great,[13] Alain of Lille,[14] and Raymond of Sabunde.[15] Again, there are some

---

[1] *Dial.*, IV, 3; Migne, *Patr. Lat.*, vol. LXXVII, col. 321.

[2] Quoted by Scotus Erigena, *De div. nat.*, V, 20; Migne, *Patr. Lat.*, vol. CXXII, col. 893.

[3] *De fide*, II, xii; Migne, *Patr. Gr.*, vol. XCIV, col. 926.

[4] *De oper. 6 dierum;* Migne, *Patr. Lat.*, vol. CLXXXIX, col. 1528 b, ff.

[5] *De immort. anim.*, ed. G. Bulow (*Beitrage zur Gesch. der Phil. des Mittelalt.*, vol. II, Münster, 1897), pp. 24–26.

[6] *Summa. theol.*, I, qu. 91, art. 1.

[7] *De hom. opific.*, XVI, 1, 2; Migne, *Patr. Gr.*, vol. XLIV, col. 180; *cf. In Psalmos*, I, iii—Migne, *ibid.*, col. 440.

[8] F. Brightman, *Liturgies Eastern and Western* (Oxford, 1896), pp. xxviii, 16.

[9] *De ambiguis* XXXVII; quoted by Scotus Erigena, *De div. nat.*, V, 20.

[10] *Op. cit.*, II, 4; Migne, *Patr. Lat.*, vol. CXXII, col. 530.

[11] *Ibid.*, IV, 10, col. 782–785; *cf.* II, 4, col. 530, and III, 37, col. 733.

[12] *De fide*, II, xii.

[13] *Homil. in Evang.*, II, 29; Migne, *Patr. Lat.*, vol. LXXVI, col. 1214.

[14] *De planctu naturæ;* Migne, *Patr. Lat.*, vol. CCX, col. 443; *Distinctiones dict. theol.*, Migne, *ibid.*, col. 755.

[15] *Theol. nat.*, titles, 1, 104, 221, quoted by J. Scheuderlein, *Raymond von Sabunde* (Leipzig, 1898), pp. 12–15. *Cf.* Erdmann, *Hist. of Phil.*, I, pp. 528, 613.

comparisons between God, or world forces or processes, on the one hand, and the faculties and powers of man on the other. Gregory of Nyssa, in spite of his criticism of the view that man is a little world, thought that from the fact of order in man one might, with the aid of the microcosmic theory and its emphasis on inner knowledge, infer the existence of an immaterial soul, just as from the fact of order in the world one inferred the existence of God.[1] Augustine, also, had an implied criticism of the theory that man is a microcosm, when he numbered among his confessions the fact that he had once believed that God was a vast and bright body, and that he himself was a fragment of that body;[2] but he, too, veered in the direction of microcosmic theories in his views to the effect that the human mind is an image of the Trinity—a more specifically Christian doctrine, which will be considered in the next paragraph. Nilus (d. about 430) urged one of his correspondents, as "mundus mundi," to look within himself rather than upon the things of the outer world.[3] David of Nerken divided the world into three categories— beings which rule, those which both rule and are ruled, and those which only are ruled; and found a similar division between human faculties— all this in the passage in which he says that, according to Democritus, man is a little world.[4] Scotus Erigena has a parallelism between the order of the heavenly bodies and the modes of knowing.[5] Alain of Lille thinks that the position of God, angels, and men in the world is paralleled by that of wisdom, will, and pleasure, respectively, in man.[6] He says also that as the motion of the firmament is from east to west, with reappearance in the east, so man's mind turns from divine to visible things and back again to the invisible.[7] Again, the oppositions of the planets are paralleled by conflicts of tendencies in man's moral struggles.[8] Godefroid of St. Victor (12th century) left a work entitled *Microcosmus*,

---

[1] *De anima et resurrec.*, Migne, *Patr. Gr.*, vol. XLVI, cols. 25, 28.

[2] *Confessions*, IV, xvi, 31.

[3] *Epist.*, II, cxix; Migne, *Patr. Gr.*, vol. LXXIX, col. 252.

[4] *Prolegomena*, XII: ed. A. Busse (in *Commentaria in Aristotelem græca*, vol. XVIII, Berlin, 1904), p. 34.

[5] *De div. nat.*, IV, 10; Migne, *Patr. Lat.*, vol. CXXII, col. 783.

[6] *De planctu naturæ;* Migne, *Patr. Lat.*, vol. CCX, col. 444. *Dist. dict. theol;* Migne, *ibid.*, col. 866.

[7] *Ibid.*, col. 866.

[8] *De planctu nat.*; Migne, *ibid.*, col. 443. *Dist. dict. theol.*, col. 866. For views of Alain, see M. Baumgartner, *Die Phil. des Alanus de Insul.*, in *Beitrage zur Gesch. der Phil. des Mittelalters*, vol. II (Münster, 1898), pp. 88 ff. There are references to other mediæval writers, p. 88, n. 3.

in which the four elements were compared to four faculties of the soul.[1]
Theories to the effect that man's body or some part of it is similar in
structure to the universe or some part of it are found in Ambrose and
Synesius. The former says that the world is framed like man's body; as
in man the head, so in the world, the sky is the most excellent member;
and as the eyes in man, so are the sun and moon.[2] Synesius compared
man's spherical head to the stars, and thought that the heads of men,
the domiciles of their souls, were "in the world little worlds." [3] Several
writers held that to the four elements in the world corresponded the four
"humours," or bodily fluids, in man. Among these was Isidorus His-
palensis, who calls man "another world, created from the universality of
things in abbreviated fashion," [4] and interprets John I, 10—"the world
knew him not"—as a reference to the microcosmic theory.[5] The Vener-
able Bede held that the correspondence between elements and humors
extended also to the four seasons.[6] Honorius of Autun (twelfth century)
thought that to the seven planets with their music corresponded the
seven notes of the scale and also man, with the four elements in his body
and the three powers of his soul! [7] Among the Christian writers, Synesius [8] and the author of the *Dialogue concerning Astrology* which comes
to us under the name of Hermippus,[9] thought that there was enough
correspondence between various portions of the universe to make divination or astrology possible. The latter thinks that the distribution of
planetary influences throughout the human body is in line with the
doctrine which says that man is a little world on earth.[10]

---

[1] J. Haureau, *Hist. de la philos. scolastique* (Paris, 1872), vol. I, p. 515.

[2] *Hexamæron*, VI, ix, 55; Migne, *Patr. Lat.*, vol. XIV, col. 265.

[3] *De providentia*, I. Quoted by Gataker on M. Aurelius, *De rebus suis*, IV, 27. Something similar is found in the *De mundi creatione* of Severian (5th century), Orat. I;
Migne, *Patr. Gr.*, vol. LVI, col. 443.

[4] *Sententiarum*, I, viii, 1, 2; Migne, *Patr. Lat.*, vol. LXXXIII, col. 549.

[5] *De natura rerum*, IX, 2; Migne, *ibid.*, col. 978. The Greek term is here given as one
word, μικρόκοσμος. Meyer (op. cit., p. 98) says that R. Eucken (*Gesch. der philos.
Terminol.*, p. 35) traces this form to Bœthius.

[6] *De temporum ratione*, XXXV; Migne, *Patr. Lat.*, vol. XC, col. 458. In this passage
the transliteration "microcosmos" appears as one word.

[7] *De imagine mundi*, I, lxxxii; Migne, *Patr. Lat.*, vol. CLXXII, col. 140. In this passage the Greek term is given as μικρόκοσμος.

[8] *De insomniis*, II, III.

[9] W. Kroll and P. Viereck, in their (Teubner) edition (Leipzig, 1895) date this work
in the 5th–6th century (p. v).

[10] *Ibid.*, I, xiii, 81. *Cf.* Bouché-Leclercq, *L'astrol. grecq.*, p. 78, n. 1.

*5. Some Developments More Distinctively Christian.* In some cases the Christian writers exhibit something more than a mere repetition of views essentially Greek. First among these may be noted Augustine's doctrine to the effect that in human nature is the image of the Trinity. He gives various reasons for this view—because of the facts that we are, and know that we are, and delight in our being and knowledge; [1] or, again, because of the mind's possession of memory, understanding, and will.[2] He also discerns an image of the Trinity in the threefold division of knowledge into physical, logical and ethical branches.[3] After Augustine, Anselm held that the mind, since it is capable of remembering and conceiving and loving itself, is an image of the Trinity.[4] Augustine also has the famous parallelism between the seven periods of human (Old and New Testament) history [5] and the ages of man—given variously as six,[6] or seven.[7] Augustine sees one defect in the scheme, in that it makes Christ come in a period of history which corresponds to old age in the life of an individual, instead of that which corresponds to youth; but he says that conditions differ somewhat in the race and the individual, and that "youth" refers to the vigor of man's faith.[8] There is a suggestion of microcosmic theories in the mystical writings of Pseudo-Dionysius, who delineates the celestial and ecclesiastical hierarchies, each composed of triads,[9] and declares that it is possible to find within each of the parts of our bodies heavenly virtues which are images of the angelic. Analogies and symbols are specified for the senses, the organs of the body, meteorological processes, animal species, fire, and so on, in this connecting link between Neo-Platonism and the later Christian mysticism.[10] Isidore of Pelusium (about 450) interpreted the last verse of the Gospel of John in terms of the microcosmic theory.[11] Another speculation which may have served as a prototype of the work of some later thinkers is found in the *Policraticus* of John of Salisbury, who declares that the prince is the head of a state,[12] and the image of the Deity.[13] In obeying a prince we follow the leading of nature which has placed all the senses of man, the

---

[1] *Civ. Dei*, XI, xxvi; *cf. De Trin.*, IX, iii and iv.
[2] *De Trin.*, X, xi, 17.　　[3] *Civ. Dei*, XI, xxv.　　[4] *Monol.*, LXVII.
[5] *De Genes. contra Manich.*, I, xxiii, 35–41.
[6] *De vera religione*, XXVI, 48.　　[7] *De quant. anim.*, XXXIII, 70–74.
[8] *Retract.*, I, 26; *cf. De div. quæst.*, LXXXIII, qu. 44.
[9] See H. O. Taylor, art., Dionys. Areop., in *Encyc. Brit.* (11), vol. VIII, p. 285.
[10] *Celestial Hierarchy*, XV; Migne, *Patr. Gr.*, vol. III, col. 326.
[11] *Epist.*, I, 259; Migne, *Patr. Gr.*, vol. LXXVIII, col. 338.
[12] *Policraticus*, V, vi.　　[13] *Ibid.*, VI, xxv.

microcosm, in the head, and subjected the other members to it.[1]  The
senate constitutes the heart of a state; the guards of the provinces, its
eyes, ears, and tongue; [2] the army and judiciary, its hands; [3] and those
who do the menial tasks, its feet.[4]  According to O. Gierke this was the
first attempt [5] to find some portion of the body which would correspond
to each portion of the state.  Thus some of the microcosmic theories
persisted in later times in something of the form given them by the
mediæval Christian thinkers; but they were not of great importance for
the Christian system.  The data from the microcosmic theories may be
said, like the evidence from so many other fields, to indicate that the
interests of Christianity at this time were chiefly other-worldly, and
concerned more with escaping from the world than with picturing men
as members of it.

6. *Possible Influence of Jewish and Arabian Thought upon Christian
Microcosmic Theories.*  So far as one can detect, the Christian writers
throughout the mediæval period exhibit no marked dependence upon
the Jewish and Arabian writers who were, as we shall see, working out
microcosmic theories of their own.  It is of course not possible to say that
the three developed in utter isolation; but on the other hand the occurrence of similar views in writers belonging to two different religions is not
to be taken offhand as evidence of an interchange of ideas.  More often
such similarities point to common dependence upon philosophies older
than either.  Certainly the Jewish and Arabic traditions are on broad
lines distinguishable from the Christian.  As a trace of possible influence
of one tradition on another, it may be significant that at least one of the
earliest Christian writings which use the term corresponding to " microcosm" in their titles, and the earliest Jewish writing which uses a similar
term were written within a few years of one another.  The Christian
work is entitled *De mundi universitate libri duo, sive megacosmus et microcosmus;* it was written by Bernard Silvestris (or, Bernard of Tours),[6]
perhaps in the years 1145–1153.[7]  It combines Christian, Neo-Platonic
and Pythagorean theories.[8]  In the first book it is explained that matter

[1] *Policraticus*, IV, 1.     [2] *Ibid.*, V, ix, xi.     [3] *Ibid.*, VI, 1.     [4] *Ibid.*, VI, xx.
[5] *Political Theories of the Middle Ages*, Eng. transl. F. Maitland (Cambridge, 1900),
p. 24.  Gierke interprets the political thought of the Middle Ages preëminently in
terms of macrocosm and microcosm (Sec. II).
[6] See M. De Wulf, *History of Mediæval Philosophy*, Eng. transl. by Coffey (New York,
1909), p. 181.
[7] Ueberweg et al., *Grundriss der Geschichte der Philosophie* (10th edition, Berlin, 1915),
vol. II, pp. 313–314.          [8] De Wulf, *op. cit.*, p. 220.

received its form in the four elements through the effort of the world-soul, which also placed the nine hierarchies of angels in heaven, fixed the stars and the winds, and created the living forms in their environments. In the second book man the microcosm is said to have been formed from the four elements as the completion of creation.[1] The Jewish work is entitled *Sefer Olam Katan* ("The Book of the Little World," "the Microcosm"), and is by Joseph Ibn Zaddik of Cordova, who died in 1149.[2] There seem to be no striking resemblances between the contents of the two books; the chief point of interest is in the resemblance of the titles. Possibly both go back to some Arabic works[3] similarly entitled; or possibly one imitated the other. Meyer thinks it possible that Ibn Zaddik was influenced by Bernard;[4] but the fact that Bernard uses the terms as a subtitle, and that the possible dates for his work fall partly after the accepted date of the death of Ibn Zaddik may indicate an influence in the opposite direction, if there was any influence at all. A possible connection of another kind between Arabian and Christian views has been noted by De Wulf, who says that for the great scholastics psychology forms a chapter of physics, but the most important one, because man is the microcosm and the central pivot of all nature.[5] He thinks that Gundisallinus, a connecting link between the Arabian and the scholastic philosophies,[6] gave a peripatetic meaning to the "Alexandrian" conception of man as a microcosm.[7] In his *De immortalitate animæ*, Gundisallinus says that the human soul is midway between animal souls and angelic substances, and is partly dependent upon the body and partly independent of it.[8] The incorruptible soul is not destroyed by the severing of form from matter, *i. e.*, by death.[9] The question here appears to be, not so much one of peripatetic influence upon the scholastics, as of whether De Wulf's use of the term microcosm to describe their psychology does not tend to exaggerate the place which microcosmic theories held among them.

## 3. Microcosmic Theories in Mediæval Jewish Philosophy

*1. General Characteristics of Jewish Works in this Period.* The microcosmic theories of the mediæval Jewish writers frequently contain state-

---

[1] *De mundi universitate* . . . ed. C. Barach and J. Wrobel (Innsbrück, 1876), Breviarium.

[2] See next section. [3] See sec. 4.

[4] *Op. cit.*, p. 50. [5] *Op. cit.*, p. 332. [6] *Ibid.*, p. 270. [7] *Ibid.*, p. 273.

[8] Edition of G. Bülow, cited above, pp. 24–26. [9] *Ibid.*, pp. 28–29.

ments identical with, or similar to those of the Christians, but the Jewish
treatment differs in general in at least four respects.  In the first place it
has a basis in more ancient writings—as we saw, in the *Sefer Yezirah*
and Philo, with scattered references in the Talmud and some of the Midrashim.  Secondly, microcosmic theories, while held, as in the case of the
Christians, by writers more or less obscure, are given more prominence by
the great Jewish than by the great Christian writers.  Again, the theory
that man is a microcosm is developed  much farther in the direction of
naïve and crude comparisons between the world and man.  Lastly, the
Jewish theories are if anything more closely related to the Arabian views
than are the Christian.

   2. *Theories Emphasizing Physical Resemblances between the Universe
and Man.*  We consider first a number of writers  who emphasize a
physical interpretation of Genesis I, 26, the doctrine that man was made
in the image of God.  This was early linked up with the microcosmic
theory; according to the old and valuable Midrash *Bereshit Rabba*, of the
sixth, or possibly the third century,[1] when God said, "Let *us* make man
in *our* image," it was with "the works of heaven and earth" that God
was taking counsel.[2]  This is the earliest known source for a view after-
wards held by other writers.[3]  According to the *Pirké* of Rabbi Eliezer
(eighth century [4]), man was created from four kinds of dust; from red
dust came the blood, from black the intestines, from white the bones, and
from yellow the nerves, in order that man might  reunite all, and that,
wherever he might turn, he would remember  that he was dust.  Just as
the Creator supports the universe without fatigue, so the soul supports
the body without effort.[5]  The first detailed exposition of the microcosmic theory in this period is that of the *Abot* of R. Natan (eighth or ninth
century).[6]  Starting from an older view ascribed to R. Joseph the Gal-
ilean, to the effect that God had created in man everything that had been
created in the universe, the author of this work proceeds to a detailed
parallelism, covering about thirty items.  For example, the forests
correspond to man's hair; slanderers in the world correspond to the ears
with which man hears slander; the wind corresponds to the nose with

---

[1] See *Encyc. Brit.* (11th ed.), XVIII, 423.
   [2] Translation by August Wünsche in *Bibl. rabbinica* (Leipzig, 1880), vol. I, parascha
viii, p. 31.
   [3] A. Jellinek, *Beiträge zur Geschichte der Kabbala* (1852), vol. I, p. 7, Anmerk. 6.
   [4] *Encyc. Brit.*, XVIII, 423.
   [5] S. Karppe, *Études sur . . . Zohar*, pp. 135-136.          [6] *Jewish Encyc.*, I, 82.

which man breathes; the sun, to the forehead; the sky, to the tongue—
and so on.[1]  I. Broydé, in his article in the *Jewish Encyclopædia*,[2]
quotes a few of these, but in his selection fails to indicate how haphazard
and trivial is the list.  The parallelisms, absurd as they are, have some
importance, since they suggest something of what may have been the
relations of various microcosmic traditions; they are fantastic enough to
show that they were not taken over from Greek sources, and on the other
hand are perhaps too early, as well as too crude, to have come from the
Arabian Brethren of Sincerity.  About the ninth or tenth century,
David ben Mervan al Mokammez and Jepheth ben Ali thought that man
united so many perfections in himself that he was superior even to the
angels.[3]  The latter, in his commentary on Genesis I, 25, used a term
אלעאלם אלצגיר, corresponding to the term "microcosm," which Steinschneider thinks was not first brought into Jewish literature through the
Brethren of Sincerity.[4]  Saadia ben Joseph (892–942), who has been
called the greatest figure in the literary and political history of mediæval Judaism, author of a famous commentary on the *Sefer Yezirah*,
taught that God has in the universe the rôle of life in the living organism;
or, that God might be compared to human intelligence.[5]  The earth is in
the center of the universe and is the goal of creation; and, since nothing
without reason can be the earth's goal, that goal must be man.[6]  Saadia
has a curious triple parallelism of the universe, the tabernacle, and man,
according to which the sun and moon are typified in the candlestick,
and, again, in the human eyes; and the firmament, separating the waters
above it from the waters below it, has its analogues in the veil of the
temple, and again in the human diaphragm.[7]  Shabbethai Donnolo (913–
965) wrote a work called *Man as God's Image*, repeating the old view that

---

[1] *Abot* of R. Natan, XXXI, 3 (German translation by K. Pollak, *Rabbi Nathans
System der Ethik und Moral* (Frankfurt, 1905), pp. 109–110.

[2] Article, " Microcosm," *Jewish Encyc.* VIII, 544.

[3] S. Karppe, *op. cit.*, p. 453, n.

[4] *Die Hebraïsche Übersetzungen des Mittelalters*, p. 997, n. 1.  Aḥudhemme (d. 575)
wrote a treatise upon man considered as a microcosm; R. Duval, *La litt. syriaque*
(Paris, 1900), p. 250.

[5] *Commentary on the Sefer Yezirah*, French transl. by M. Lambert (Paris, 1891),
IV, 1, pp. 91–95.

[6] J. Guttmann, *Die Religionsphilosophie des Saadia* (Göttingen, 1882), pp. 159–
160.

[7] S. Karppe, *op. cit.*, p. 171.  Such a view occurs in one of the Midrashim; see A.
Jellinek's edition of Shabbethai (Schabtai Donolo, *Der Mensch als Gottes Ebenbild*,
Introduction), p. xii.

God, in creating man in "our image," took counsel with the universe,[1] and made man not only with his body resembling the material universe, but with his soul resembling God. Both kinds of resemblances are described in detail, so that the work suggests not only structural parallelisms but also arguments for the immortality of the soul.[2] As the four elements emanated from God, in the order air, water, fire, earth, so man's body was created from four analogous humours—blood, phlegm, black bile, and yellow bile;[3] we noted that such a view was held by several Christian writers. For Shabbethai Donnolo, further, the process of human generation also affords analogues to the four elements. Moreover, man has the power to produce the four elements; he breathes and produces air; if the air meets a hard object, the latter becomes damp; man can produce fire by means of a burning-glass; and man can produce a solid mass by boiling a kettle of water a long time. Thus man can see how creation proceeded, and can himself be like God.[3] Jellinek says that this work was important, as the exegesis of Genesis I, 25 was in its main outlines taken over by a number of later writers; and that it was of considerable influence on the Cabala, since it opened the way now for spiritual as well as corporeal interpretations of the ten powers present in man, as well as for the concept of the Adam Kadmon, or typical, cosmic man.[4] But the last-named has affiliations with much older sources, like the *Poimandres*. Before passing on to some of these other emphases, it should be noted that in the *Midrash of the Microcosm*, the title of which Jellinek traces to Arabic influences, the theory of physical parallelisms between the universe and man is treated in a manner which recalls the *Abot* of Rabbi Natan, although the detail of the parallelisms suggests some independence on the part of the author.[5]

3. *Theories Emphasizing Metaphysical Resemblances between the Universe and Man.* Whether because of the influence of Shabbethai Donnolo's twofold exegesis of the passage in Genesis, or because of the influence of the Arabian philosophers now beginning to be felt, or as the developments of independent views, there follow now a number of writers who emphasize metaphysical rather than physical resemblances between the universe and man. Of these, a notable figure is Solomon Ibn

---

[1] Jellinek, *ibid.*, p. ix.

[2] *Ibid.*, p. x.

[3] *Ibid.*, pp. x, xi.

[4] *Ibid.*, p. xii.

[5] A. Jellinek, *Bet-ha Midrasch*, 5-ten Teil (Vienna, 1873), Introduction, p. xxv.

Gabirol (Avicebron, 1021–1058). Like the Arabian Brethren, he declares that if man wishes to know all things he must first know himself.[1] The body of man and his form exemplify matter and form; his soul exemplifies (cosmic) will; and his intelligence exemplifies the primal essence [2]— "mundus minor exemplum est maioris mundi ordine." [3] The spiritual substance which is said to contain the material universe is compared to the spiritual substance which is said to contain the body.[4] In both cases there is diffusion [5] and direction of movement,[6] although contamination of higher by lower is avoided by means of intermediaries.[7] The individual soul follows the order of the world.[8] Karppe comments that here is a metaphysical application of the doctrine of the microcosm which, however, was only rarely maintained at this level; [9] in another work of Ibn Gabirol there is the more usual view that man is midway between two worlds, and that his four humours correspond to the four elements.[10] After Ibn Gabirol, Moses Ibn Ezra had a theory that man was a microcosm because he resembled the universe in composition, derivation and creation; [11] Neumark says that he conceived the theory more clearly than Ibn Gabirol, from whom he derived it.[12] For Abraham Ibn Daud (d. about 1180), the process of knowing shows that man is a microcosm, since he contains in himself everything from the realm of the substantial categories, and, in his grasp of intelligible forms, is like the separate spirits.[13]

4. *Microcosmic Theories with Psychological and Ethical Emphasis: Bahya Ibn Paquda, Joseph Ibn Zaddik.* In the eleventh century, Bahya Ibn Paquda of Saragossa, author of the work called *The Duties of the Heart*, tried to combat the profane philosophy of Ibn Gabirol,[14] but he too used the theory that man is a microcosm. In order to know the universe, we must study man, in both body and soul; then much of the mystery of the universe will become clear to us. This is the meaning of

---

[1] *Fons vitæ* (Latin transl. by Gundisallinus, ed. C. Baeumker, in *Beiträge zur Gesch. der Phil. des Mittelalt.*, vol. I, Münster, 1892), I, 2.

[2] *Ibid.*, I, 7.      [3] *Ibid.*, III, ii, 10; *cf.* IV, 16.      [4] *Ibid.*, II, 24.

[5] *Ibid.*, III, 15.      [6] *Ibid.*, III, 58.      [7] *Ibid.*, II, 24; *cf.* III, ii, 10.

[8] III, 58.      [9] *Op. cit.*, p. 185.

[10] J. Guttmann, *Die Philosophie des Sal. Ibn Gabirols* (Göttingen, 1889), p. 17.

[11] *Jewish Encyc.*, VIII, 546.

[12] *Gesch. der jud. Phil. . . .*, vol. I, p. 508, n. 1.

[13] *Ibid.*, vol. I, p. 576.

[14] I. Broydé, *Resumé des reflexions sur L'âme de Bahya . . . ibn Pakouda* (Paris, 1896), pp. 3–7.

Job when he says "And from my flesh I shall see God." [1]  The minerals, plants, animals and men are pictured as belonging in a series leading up to the world of intelligences; gold, "rooted in the ground" is an intermediate link between minerals and plants; palm trees, with their process of fecundation, a link between plants and animals; many animal characteristics a link between animals and man; and prophets are links between man and the world of intelligences. [2]  Something of this kind occurs in the work of the Arabian Brethren; and it is a question whether, in view of their work, the parallels which Bahya draws between the nine spheres of the universe, the twelve signs of the Zodiac, and the seven planets, on the one hand, and various faculties and organs of the human body, on the other hand, should be designated as "very original." Broydé has made this statement; [3] but in another work has said that Bahya was a faithful imitator of the Brethren. [4]  We have noted in connection with Bernard Silvestris the work of Joseph Ibn Zaddik (d. 1149), called *The Book of the Microcosm*. [5]  Against various forms of indifference and materialism current in his day, he argues for the unity of God and the way to true knowledge; [6] and the microcosmic theory serves him as a convenient means to this end. [7]  Man, representing as he does in his body the entire material universe, and in his soul the entire world of spirits, should know himself in order that he may know the will of God, and see that God alone is truth. [8]  In particular, he should know that God's act of creating the world was immediate, and did not begin by a preliminary creation of the divine will. [9]  In the working out of the argument, the soul of man is compared with the world-soul; the vegetable, animal, and rational souls have their ground in three corresponding world-souls, and the individualized intelligence has its ground in universal intelligence. [10]  In his body, man has the properties of the four elements, for he goes from heat to cold, from wetness to dryness. [11]  The heavenly sphere corresponds

---

[1] *Duties of the Heart*, Eng. transl. by E. Collins (*Wisdom of the East* series, London, 1905), pp. 40–41.

[2] Broydé, *Resumé*, p. 12.

[3] Broydé, *Jewish Encyc.*, VIII, 544.     [4] *Resumé*, p. 16.

[5] . . . ספר עולם הקטן, edited by Jellinek (Berlin, 1854).   On the Hebrew title, cf. M. Doctor, *Die Philosophie des Josef (Ibn) Zaddik* . . . (in *Beiträge zur Gesch. der Phil. des Mittelalt.*, vol. II, Münster, 1898), p. 3.

[6] B. Beer, p. 200 (article cited in Introduction, above).

[7] *Ibid.*, p. 163; cf. M. Doctor, *op. cit.*, p. 19.

[8] Beer, *op. cit.*, pp. 163, 199; Doctor, *op. cit.*, pp. 18–21.

[9] Doctor, *op. cit.*, p. 47.     [10] Doctor *op. cit.*, pp. 30–31.     [11] *Ibid.*, p. 20.

to man's head; [1] to the four elements correspond four senses. [2]   In man
are accumulated the processes and powers observable in all mineral,
vegetable, and animal species.   Man's hair is like grass, his veins and
arteries like rivers and canals, and his bones like mountains.   In his
qualities also he resembles various animals, uniting all their qualities in
himself. [3]   The parallels remind one strongly of the Arabian Brethren;
but Ibn Zaddik has some—*e. g.*, the comparison of the days of the solar
month to the teeth!—which are apparently original. [4]   There have been
a number of theories regarding the affiliations of Ibn Zaddik.   Maimonides is read in one passage as having thought that he was one of the
Brethren of Sincerity. [5]   Jellinek thinks there are traces of Bahya Ibn
Paquda's influence, [6] while P. Block thinks that Ibn Zaddik depended
upon Ibn Gabirol. [7]   Doctor thinks that any direct dependence either
upon the Brethren or Ibn Gabirol is uncertain except that in his microcosmic views he must have used one or the other. [8]   L. Weinsberg has
questioned the authenticity of the whole work, which he thinks appeared
in the thirteenth century. [9]   According to De Wulf, Ibn Zaddik's book
marks a transition between the theological philosophy of the orthodox
Mohammedans (the Motakallimin) and the Jewish Aristotelianism of
Maimonides. [10]   The book was used by a number of later Jewish writers. [11]

5. *Maimonides.*   The great Moses ben Maimun (1135–1204) in his
*Moreh Nebuchim*, or "Guide for the Perplexed"—an effort to show by
philosophy the reasonableness of the faith—combined all these tendencies, but with an emphasis upon physical resemblances between the

---

[1] L. Weinsberg, *Der Mikrokosmos: Ein angeblich in 12. Jahrhund. von J. Ibn Zaddik
verfasstes phil. System.* (Breslau, 1888), p. 54, n. 3.

[2] Beer, *op. cit.*, p. 194.

[3] Doctor, *op. cit.*, p. 20.

[4] *Cf. ibid.*, and Weinsberg, *loc. cit.*

[5] Neumark, *op. cit.*, I, 389; *cf.* Weinsberg. *op. cit.*, p. 46.

[6] *Der Mikrokosmos*, Introduction, p. vii.

[7] *Die Religionsphilosophie der Juden*, in J. Winter and A. Wünsche, *Gesch. der rabb.
Lit. wahrend des Mittelalt.* (Leipzig, 1892–5), vol. II, p. 729.

[8] *Op. cit.*, pp. 16, 19.

[9] *Op. cit.*, pp. 46–48. Weinsberg bases his claim upon a statement of Maimonides
(p. 12), and upon the facts that "Ibn Zaddik," contrary to the implications of Maimonides, differs at various points from both Arabians (p. 14, ff.) and Aristotelians
(p. 27, ff.), and agrees with the orthodox Mohammedan theologians (p. 39, ff.). Weinsberg has made a good study of the material, but depended too much upon statements
which might easily be otherwise construed, or even be erroneous.

[10] *Hist. of Mediæval Phil.*, p. 238.          [11] Jellinek, *op. cit.*, Introd., p. viii.

universe and man which was not blind to their limitations. For him, as for Ibn Zaddik, microcosmic theories helped to demonstrate the unity of God.[1] He gives a detailed parallelism between the universe and the human body. Each is an individual; as the universe is composed of spheres and their parts, primary and subordinate, the body is composed of organs and their parts, primary and subordinate. The spheres have life and soul, if not intellect. The outer sphere, enclosing the four inner spheres of the elements, corresponds to the human heart—especially in the fact that if it ceases to function, destruction ensues. The revolution of the spheres corresponds to the process of change in finite substance. Just as the universe has some parts without motion or life, so the body has some parts devoid of motion and sensation. In each, we find that one part cannot exist without other parts; there is in each a force which unites and preserves the various parts. Again, in each, some parts have special purposes, others are merely accessory; and, in each, it is the latter only which may exhibit great variations in size. In each, there is some substance—*i. e.*, the "fifth element,"—which exists permanently in individuation; and in each there are other substances (*i. e.*, the four elements, the four humours), which are constant only in the species. Just as the heavenly spheres, penetrating the combinations of elements, may move them and at last by the same force cause their destruction, so the same force which operates in the birth and temporal existence of the human being operates in his destruction and death. In the universe, the nearer the parts are to the center, the greater is the turbidness, inertness; in the animals, the vital organs are nearest the center.[2] In a passage suggesting the criticism by Gregory of Nyssa, Maimonides says that none of the foregoing analogies justifies the calling of man a microcosm, any more than of a horse. It is the intellectual faculty—which by the way is pictured as socially elicited—which raises man to that dignity. The force in man which directs him is the analogue of God in the universe. One might say that the absolute intellect of man, acquired from without, is the analogue of God, and that man's rational faculties represent the intelligence of the spheres; but Maimonides thinks these latter comparisons involve too many disputed questions.

Maimonides is perhaps the first writer who clearly enumerates objections to the microcosmic theory. Whereas in man the benefits of organs

---

[1] *The Guide for the Perplexed*, Eng. transl. by M. Friedlander (London, 1910), Part I, chapter LXXII, p. 115.

[2] *Ibid.*, pp. 113–119.

subordinate to the heart also benefit the heart, in the universe that outer sphere which bestows authority and distributes power does not receive any benefit, but merely imitates the Most High. In man, again, the heart is internal, and in the universe its analogue is the outmost sphere. Moreover, the faculty of thinking is inherent in man's body, and inseparable from it, while God is not inherent in the universe and may exist apart from it.[1] Apart from man, the four spheres correspond to the four elements—that of the moon, to water; of the sun, to fire; of the five planets, to air; and of the fixed stars, to earth—and also to the four powers of the sublunar world, the four causes of motion in the spheres—*i. e.*, Nature, Soul, Intelligence, and abstract Spirit—and the four stages of Jacob's Ladder.[2] Thus, in spite of some objections in the matter of physical parallelisms, microcosmic theories became an integral part of the world-view of the greatest of Jewish philosophers. Of immense influence within Judaism, Maimonides was also read in part by Christian schoolmen.[3]

*6. Microcosmic Theories in the "Cabala."* In the thirteenth century microcosmic theories from the *Sefer Yezirah* and other sources were gathered up and given a mystical direction in the *Cabala.*[4] According to the *Zohar*, one of the two great cabalistic text-books, everything emanates from the Ain Soph (Infinite) or Primal Spirit, whose first manifestation is the prototypal cosmic man, Adam Kadmon.[5] From the latter emanates the created universe in four degrees, or worlds. The first world consists of the ten operative powers or qualities of the Adam Kadmon, combining the sacred numbers 3 and 7. From this first world emanate the three other worlds, those of life, spirit, and intelligence,[6] each divided into ten subordinate spheres.[7] Everything which the Adam Kadmon contains virtually, man contains actually; man participates in the three created worlds,[8] to which the three powers of man's soul correspond. When man was created, all the spheres coöperated; they could not exist, in fact, without man to bind them together.[9] The human body is the model of

---

[1] *Ibid.*, pp. 117–119.

[2] *Ibid.*, chapter IX; *cf.* Neumark, *op. cit.* I, 601–602.

[3] *Encyc. Brit.* (11th ed.), XIII, 173.

[4] *Encyc. Brit.*, XIII, 174; Karppe, *op. cit.*, p. 452.

[5] S. Munk, *Mélanges de philosophie juive et arabe* (Paris, 1859), p. 492.

[6] J. Probst, *Caractère et origine des idées de R. Lulle* (Toulouse, 1912), pp. 234–235.

[7] E. Bischoff, *Die Kabbalah* (Leipzig, 1903), p. 55.

[8] Munk, *op. cit.*, p. 493.

[9] Karppe, *op. cit.*, pp. 455–456.

all the creations.[1]  The vault of heaven corresponds to man's skin; the constellations to the skin's configuration; the four elements to man's flesh, and the internal forces of the universe (*i. e.*, angels and servants of God), to man's bones and veins.[2]  According to Beer, it was from the Cabalists that the idea that man is the image of all things in the universe passed to the Christian mystics and theosophists of the sixteenth and seventeenth centuries; [3] but the latter certainly had much in their own traditions.

#### 4. MICROCOSMIC THEORIES IN MOHAMMEDAN PHILOSOPHY

*1. Two Streams of Greek Tradition.*  We have seen that some of the conceptions of Greek philosophy spread, by way of Alexandria, through the west, where they were absorbed and carried along in the currents of patristic and scholastic Christian thinking.  There was another stream of Greek tradition, which proceeded by way of Byzantium to the east,[4] where its teachings were absorbed by the Arabians in the days of Mohammedan ascendancy, and conserved until, centuries later, they also came to the west, by way of the Mohammedan dominions in Spain.  In the meantime, the Greek conceptions were modified by the Arabs; and one of the chief modifications was in the direction of a more consistent and more prominent theory of man as a microcosm.

*2. The "Brethren of Sincerity."*  This modification was effected chiefly by the so-called "Ikhwan-al-Safa," or "Brethren of Sincerity," a religious society formed at Basra about 950,[5] in a time of social and ethical upheaval, with the purpose of contributing some elements of stability to a distressing national and religious situation.  It was felt that nothing could better serve this end than a unified world-view, a reconciliation of science with the true faith.  Accordingly, the Brethren prepared an *Encyclopædia*, consisting of fifty-one treatises.[6]  Dieterici says that the work constitutes a kind of supplement to the Koran, and that it has borrowed from various ancient schools of thought; the physics and logic

---

[1] Broydé, *Jewish Encyc.*, VIII, 545.          [2] Karppe, *op. cit.*, p. 454.

[3] *Op. cit.*, p. 161.

[4] F. Dieterici, *Die Philosophie der Araber in IX-ten und X-ten Jahrhünderten n. C.* (Leipzig, 1858–1895), I, 85.

[5] On possible Indian influences involved, see Neumark, *op. cit.*, I, 147; von Lippmann, *op. cit.*, p. 369.  On political motives of the Society, see T. J. De Boer, *Hist. of Philos. in Islam*, Eng. transl. E. R. Jones (London, 1903), pp. 81, ff.

[6] Dieterici, *op. cit.*, I, pp. 85–88, II, 203.  The treatises are listed in I, 131, ff.

are chiefly Aristotelian; the psychology and anthropology depend mostly upon Galen; the questions of the origin and development of the world are answered in a way suggesting Neo-Platonism and Neo-Pythagorean-ism; and the foundation of the astronomy and astrology is the teachings of Ptolemy.[1]  Two of the fifty-one treatises are entitled in terms of the microcosmic theory—the twenty-fifth, on *The Saying of the Wise, that Man is a Little World*, and the thirty-third, on *The Saying of the Wise, that the World is a Great, Good Man, Endowed with Spirit and Soul*.[2] Throughout the *Encyclopædia* the microcosmic theory is so prominent that Dieterici divides his translation and commentary into two parts called *Makrokosmos* and *Mikrokosmos*, devoted respectively to the development of the world from Unity (God) to multiplicity (things), and the reascent, in man, from multiplicity to Unity.[3]

*3. The Setting of the Microcosmic Arguments of the "Encyclopædia."* The general framework of the *Encyclopædia's* world-view is emanation-istic.  There is a well-defined attempt to express the relations between successive emanations by means of the relations between numbers in the decimal notation.  The world-soul is like unity; the simple souls represent digits; the souls of the genera, tens; those of species, hundreds, and those of individuals, thousands.  Since the nature of things corresponds to numbers, the world can consist of only nine stages.[4]  Of these the four spiritual stages are God, Reason, Soul and Primary Matter.  The inter-mediate stages are Secondary Matter, and the World.  The lower stages are Nature; the Four Elements; and the "Products," mineral, vegetable, and animal.  By the addition of an encircling sphere to the sphere of the fixed stars, the spheres of the five planets and of the sun and the moon, the world, in its turn, was made to consist of nine spheres, or divisions;[5] but this arrangement gives way to others involving only the

---

[1] Dieterici, *op. cit.*, VIII, 208.

[2] For the Arabic titles, see G. Flügel, "Über Inhalt und Verfasser der Arabischen Encyclopædie," in *Zeitschr. d. Deutsch. Morgenländ. Gesellschaft*, xiii, pp. 11 and 13, Anm. 3. (Leipzig, 1859).

[3] *Op. cit.*, I, p. v, and p. 10. The *Encyclopædia* does not hold strictly to the micro-cosmic theory in the sense in which we have taken it; there are a number of passages in which metaphorical and allegorical comparisons of man and other parts of the universe are introduced—*e. g.*, the twenty-second treatise (VII, 1 ff.) compares man to a city, and even the treatises mentioned above include other comparisons than the microcosmic. (See VII, 43 ff., VIII, 29 ff.) Dieterici's translation has been criticized as fragmentary and inexact; see von Lippmann, *op. cit.*, p. 369, n. 21 (370).

[4] Dieterici, *op. cit.*, I, 163; VIII, 31.     [5] *Ibid.*, I, pp. 163–179.

seven last-named. The spheres brood over the elements; [1] or, the world-soul works through the motions of the stars upon the elements and products; [2] by mixtures of the elements, minerals, plants, animals and men are produced.[3] The fiftieth treatise gives an arrangement of minerals, plants and animals in the order of their appearance, with transition stages between the three; it is declared that fungi are intermediate between plants and minerals, and that date-palms are intermediate between plants and animals. Again, the monkey has a body like that of man, and the horse and elephant have traits of disposition like man.[4] This view of the world process is significant in relation to microcosmic theories for two reasons: first, because parallels are pointed out between various parts of the universe, especially between the universe and man, and second because the essentials of the whole process are viewed as concentrated in the end-product, man.[5]

*4. The "Encyclopædia's" Parallelisms between the Universe and Man.* The parallelisms between the universe and man are worked out in much more detail than in any previous works. Among them are the statements that, as God knows the secrets of all worlds, so the human soul knows what each of the senses separately knows.[6] As the spiritual powers (angels, etc.) penetrate the universe, the powers of the soul penetrate the human body.[7] As the world is divided into nine concentric spheres, so the human body is divided into nine regions or substances, grouped in concentric fashion.[8] The world is cone-shaped; the earth, as well as most fruits and human products, being cone-shaped or round, repeats the pattern.[9] There are twelve signs of the Zodiac, six northerly and six southerly; there are twelve openings in the body, of which six are said to be on the right side and six on the left. Again, there are seven planets through which the determinations of heaven are communicated to the earth; and there are seven creative powers through which the welfare of the body is established. Or, as another parallel to the seven planets, there are seven spiritual powers—the five senses, together with thinking and reasoning. The relation which the moon sustains to the sun is sustained

[1] *Ibid.*, VIII, p. 16.        [2] *Ibid.*, I, p. 187.        [3] *Ibid.*, VIII, p. 16.

[4] These views resemble those of Bahya Ibn Paquda, noted above. Ibn Paquda modifies the statement about the date-palm, giving a better example of a characteristic common to that and the animals. The *Encyclopædia* says that the date-palm, though shaped like a plant, dies if one cuts its head off, and hence may be said to have an animal soul. See Dieterici, IX, pp. 219 ff.

[5] *Ibid.*, VIII, p. 16, ff.        [6] *Ibid.*, VII, p. 57.

[7] VII, pp. 47, 57; *cf.* V, pp. 2, 4–8.        [8] VII, p. 47.        [9] IX, p. 216.

by the power of speech to that of reason—the moon's period of 28 days corresponds to the 28 letters of the alphabet.[1] Once more, each of the planets corresponds to an organ, as well as to an opening of the body.[2] And to each planet, further, corresponds a geographical region on earth, with its characteristic race,[3] a class of angels,[4] a month in the life of the human embryo,[5] a period of man's life, a human characteristic,[6] and a color![7] Another number which recurs over and over is that of the elements, four; it corresponds to the four principal divisions of the body,[8] and to four senses.[9] The four fundamental attributes, hot, cold, moist, dry, correspond to four bodily secretions[10] and to the four temperaments.[11] Still more detailed is the long parallelism between the structure of the earth and the structure of the human body; the mountains are said to correspond to man's bones, the minerals to marrow, the sea to the interior of the body, rivers to intestines, brooks to arteries, plants to the hair, cultural centers to the front of the body, the wilderness to the back, and so on. There are, further, detailed parallelisms between world processes and periods and bodily processes and periods—the wind and breathing, thunder and speaking, sunshine and laughter, rain and weeping, sadness and night, death and sleep, spring and childhood, summer and youth, autumn and middle life, winter and old age, the rising of stars and birth, the setting of stars and death.[12] The parallelisms are carried into social and ethical relationships when it is said that the regular course of the stars corresponds to good standing on the part of men, and retrograde motions to mistakes, and "stars standing still" to stagnation in men's work, and stars rising or passing toward the horizon to the success or failure of men.[12] Agreements and harmonies among the stars are paralleled by human loves,[13] conjunctions by union of the sexes, constellations by society, the breaking up of a star group by human separations.[14] As the stars unite with the sun and receive light, so men join with a king and receive honors; the relation of a king to his counsellors is also paralleled by the relation of the soul to the powers of sensation and other powers, and by the relation of the sun to the planets.[15] There are one or two parallelisms specifically Mohammedan; it is declared that just as the five separate senses have reference to the one soul,

---

[1] VII, pp. 48, 49.    [2] VII, pp. 49 ff., 60 ff.
[3] I, p. 208.    [4] I, p. 188.    [5] VII, p. 67 ff.
[6] VII, pp. 92–94.    [7] V, p. 115.    [8] VII, p. 50.    [9] VII, p. 189.
[10] VII, pp. 50–51.    [11] II, p. 90.    [12] VII, p. 51.    [13] VIII, p. 75.
[14] VII, pp. 51–52.    [15] VII, pp. 52, 55, 56.

so the followers of the five prophets shall all be brought before the one
Allah,[1] and again, that the angels in the upper world correspond to the
readers of the Koran, since all that the latter hear is elevated and spiritual.[2]

   *5. The Cumulation of Natural Processes in Man.*  It is declared that if
the reasonable man will reflect upon the forces which the *Encyclopædia*
describes, and come to know them, this will all be to him evidence for
his own soul, and an indication of the nature of man.[3]  In the composition
of man is the essence of everything which exists;[4] in body he is like the
universe, in soul he resembles the world-soul.[5]  Man is short-lived, but he
can know the whole world in himself.[6]  He shares the attributes of all
species; he has four natures and undergoes change like the four elements,
arises and disappears like the minerals, grows like the plants, has sensation and movement like the animals; "it is also possible that he is immortal like the angels."  The different animals have special ways of
seeking food and dealing with enemies, but man has all these ways
combined.  It is declared that the characteristics of some thirty species of
animals are all found in man.[7]  By reason of all this that has been noted,
"the wonderful organization of man's body, the unique processes of his
soul, the arts and sciences which arise in connection with his structure,
taken as a whole, his characters, views, ways of teaching and of acting,
words and deeds, condition, and bodily and spiritual accomplishments,"
it is fitting that man be called a little world.[8]  One should think of man's
body as of a book filled with wisdom.  If one does not know how to read
the book, one should ascertain from the Brethren the way to obtain this
true knowledge which leads to eternal life.  About the teachings of the
Brethren there need be no doubt, "for the evidence is drawn from your
own soul."[9]

   *6. The Place of the "Encyclopædia" in the History of Microcosmic
Theories.*  In spite of its naïve and fantastic views, one may say that it is
in the *Encyclopædia* of the Brethren of Sincerity that the theory that
man is a microcosm first becomes imposing.  It is no longer fragmentary,
but fundamental; and it is no longer isolated, but linked up with a comprehensive and correlated world-system.  In particular, the *Encyclopædia* is notable for its detailed parallelisms between the universe and
man; of all who have written on man as a microcosm, only Fechner has

---

[1] VII, p. 54.        [2] VII, p. 189.        [3] VII, p. 57.
[4] VII, pp. 41–42.    [5] VII, p. 60.        [6] VII, p. 46.        [7] VII, pp. 58–59.
[8] VII, p. 60; *cf.* VII, p. 41, VIII, p. 16.            [9] VII, p. 60.

tried to point out more resemblances. It should be noted also that the
Brethren have something more than a mere mention of the universe as a
"large man." Most of the writers have estimated man in terms of the
universe, but have not gone far in describing the universe in terms of
man; even where the two have been set in parallel, the direction of
emphasis has been chiefly toward man rather than away from him. The
latter undertaking is even more precarious than the former, and it is not
surprising that in their treatise on the subject the authors of the *Encyclopædia* presently wandered from macrocosmic constructions to
metaphors. Again, it was significant that terms signifying the microcosmic theories had been used as titles, even though it cannot be definitely shown that the Jewish and Christian writers who use such titles
took them from this source. Steinschneider [1] thinks that the Jews had
the term, or one corresponding to it, among themselves; and certainly in
Jewish thought there are resemblances to Philo and the *Sefer Yezirah*
which should be taken into account. With these in mind it appears un-
necessary to assume any very direct influence of the *Encyclopædia* upon
the *Cabala*. The *Encyclopædia* is, rather, a striking formulation of ideas
that, as we have seen, were more or less common to Alexandrian, Christian, Jewish, and Mohammedan writers.

*7. Related Views of Other Arabian Philosophers.* Apart from the
Brethren of Sincerity, the microcosmic theories are not conspicuous in
mediæval Arabian philosophy, although the peripatetic theory of
spheres and sphere-spirits, particularly as applied to psychology,[2] can
easily be regarded as implying something of the kind. In metaphysics,
also, there are some affiliations not very remote, as when El Farabi
taught that to the six non-corporeal principles correspond the six kinds
of bodies—the heavenly bodies, man, animal, plant, mineral, and the
four elements.[3] The Spirit which stands above us and which has lent to
all earthly things their forms, seeks to bring those scattered forms together that they may become one in love, and first collects them in man.[4]
Avicenna is more Platonic; he draws a comparison between the miracu-

---

[1] *Die Hebr. Übersetz* . . . p. 997, n. 1. *Cf.* A. Jellinek, *Bet-ha Midrasch*, 5-ten Teil
(Vienna, 1873), p. xxv, and Broydé, in *Jewish Encyclopædia*, VIII, 544.

[2] Neumark, *op. cit.*, I, 566. Traces of microcosmic views are found in a number of
obscure writers. *Cf.* Sharastani, *Religionspartheien* . . . (transl. T. Haarbrucker,
Halle, 1850), I, 169, 210.

[3] Neumark, *op. cit.*, I, 157.

[4] De Boer, *op. cit.*, p. 120.

lous effects of the world-soul and the exceptional effects of passionate forms of excitement in the human soul.[1]

### 5. SUMMARY: MICROCOSMIC THEORIES IN THEOLOGICAL TRADITIONS

The mediæval Christian writers transmitted, while the Jewish and Mohammedan writers elaborated in some fantastic details, the ancient views of man as a microcosm. In the two traditions first named the theory was usually linked up with the sacred literature and made easier the comparison between God and man.[2] For the Christians, chiefly interested in other doctrines, the microcosmic theory is hardly more than a survival; for the Jewish writers it has somewhat more importance, especially as a means to the unification of knowledge and the edification of faith. Among the Mohammedans the theory achieved importance in one sect, the Brethren of Sincerity, who as early as the tenth century held it as an integral part of a great system of philosophy. The three traditions apparently developed in considerable independence of one another, although some cases of interaction, especially between Jewish and Arabian writers, are fairly evident. In general, during the middle ages the microcosmic theory served as a convenient and uncritical method of reconciling religion with the natural sciences, which even then were beginning to raise questions and difficulties for the faithful.

[1] De Boer, *op. cit.*, p. 138.
[2] See D. Kaufmann, *Gesch. der Attributenlehre* . . . (Gotha, 1877), p. 210.

# CHAPTER III

## MICROCOSMIC THEORIES IN EARLY MODERN REACTIONS FROM SCHOLASTICISM

### 1. NEW APPLICATIONS OF THE THEORY THAT MAN IS A MICROCOSM

It is only when measured over considerable periods, or in the works of very great men, that marked differences between mediæval and modern philosophy are to be distinguished. The reaction against scholasticism in the early modern period was not sharp, but gradual; particularly in their views of man as a microcosm, some of the "modern" men differed but little from their mediæval, or even their ancient predecessors.[1] Even the men who were opening new lines of thought did not altogether forsake the old; moreover, the theory that man is a microcosm fitted well with the importance which the humanists were inclined to ascribe to man. These circumstances, combined with the fact that the chief characteristic of the period may be said to have been its curiosity, its restless seeking here and there along all lines of interest and activity, led some of the thinkers to develop new applications for the microcosmic view. Thus Nicholas of Cusa attempted to combine it with Christology, Paracelsus with empirical medicine, Bruno with symbolic logic and monadism, Campanella with a spiritualistic ontology, Boehme with mysticism, and others with new theories in the natural sciences. Some writers of the period, even while they criticized the older microcosmic theories, were not able to break entirely away from them, but incorporated portions of them at one point or another in their new estimates of the world.

[1] Among those who restated the older theories with little or no change were Agrippa of Nettesheim, in his compendium of magical and astrological lore called *De occulta philosophia*. Man contains everything in himself (II, 27, 36); the world is an intermediate image between God and man (II, 36); the parts of the soul have the relations of a musical harmony (II, 28); the motions of the heart correspond to those of the sun, and, diffused through the body, signify years, months, etc. (II, 17). Pico della Mirandola in his *De arte cabalistica* (Basle, 1572) held that man is the acme of creation, composed of two worlds (lib. III, 3145) and more fitted than the animals to be called a microcosm (lib. VII, chap. vi). On the work of Trithemius, see F. Hartmann, *The Life of Paracelsus* . . . (London, 1887), p. 164, n. On Pietro Pomponazzi, see A. H. Douglas, *The Philosophy of . . . Pomponazzi* (Cambridge, 1910), p. 127.

## 2. NICHOLAS OF CUSA

*1. Microcosmic Theories in the "De docta ignorantia" and the "De conjecturis."* The first outstanding figure of this period is Nicholas of Cusa. He holds that God is the absolute unity who reconciles all distinctions and contradictions.[1] The universe consists of three "worlds"—a central, spiritual world, the center of which is God and the characteristic of which is truth; a middle world, the center of which is intelligence, and which exhibits similarities or likenesses; and an outer world, the center of which is understanding, and which contains shadows. Sensation, or sensibility, is the thick shell around the last-named world. These three worlds are related to God as the numbers are related in decimal notation (the sum of the serial order 1, 2, 3, and 4 being equal to ten [2]); each world contains three orders, and each order contains three "choruses," all related as the tens, hundreds, and thousands. Man is organized in body and soul according to this pattern, with twenty-seven regions; so man comprises, in humanly limited fashion, the universe—his unity is infinity contracted in a human way.[3] It was reasonable, then, for the ancients to call man a microcosm.[4] In a relative sense it may be said that man is God, and a universe; he is likewise in a sense an angel, and an animal. But after all it is possible for only one man to stand, as it were, at the apex of humanity, at the point of completion of the universe, the point of union between God and man; and this man must be Christ, through whom salvation is attained for the rest of mankind.[5] Since man contains so much in himself, he can develop everything from his own nature; but his thoughts correspond to the forms in the divine mind.[6]

*2. The "De ludo globi."* If the *De ludo globi* stood alone, it might be difficult to separate microcosmic theories from illustrations and analogies; but when taken in connection with the works just considered, its meaning becomes more apparent. The globe before the persons of the dialogue is compared to the body, and its circular motion to the motion of the soul,

---

[1] *De doct. ignor.*, II, iv. God can thus be at once the greatest and the least. *Ibid.*, I, ii.

[2] Erdmann, *op. cit.*, I, 539.

[3] *De conjecturis*, II, xiv.

[4] *De doct. ignor.*, III, xiii. For other references see R. Falckenberg, *Grundzüge der Philosophie des Nicolaus Cusanus* (Breslau, 1880), p. 37, nn.

[5] *De conj.*, II, 14.

[6] *Ibid.* Cf. Erdmann, *op. cit.*, I, p. 540.

especially in introspection.[1]  The whole soul is in every part of the body, just as the Creator is in every part of the world; man is declared to be a microcosm because his soul corresponds to the world-soul.  The soul is an image of the Trinity.[2]  Into the mouth of the inquirer, but not that of the cardinal, is put the suggestion that the world is threefold—that the smallest world is man, the greatest,[3] God, and the great, or middle world, the universe; the cardinal contents himself here with saying that the whole is reflected in every part, and that the universe is reflected better in man than in anything else.  There is a further analogy between the relation of man to the universe and that of Bohemia to the Roman Empire.[4]  Doctrines like those considered in the preceding paragraph appear when it is said that God stands as unity, at the head of nine orders of angels; that, since $1+2+3+4=10$, this order is reconciled with that of the four elements, the four seasons, etc., and that, just as God has the form of everything in Himself, so that He may form everything, so our soul has the idea of everything in it, and thus may know everything.[5] Here, again, Christ is represented as the microcosmic center of the universe.[6]

## 3. PARACELSUS

*1. Statements of Paracelsus regarding Man as Microcosm.*  Of all who have held that man is a microcosm, no one has been more thoroughgoing and insistent than Paracelsus.  His various views all point in that direction.  He has the ancient theory that the world is composed of four elements,[7] but also the alchemistic view that everything comes from mercury, sulphur, and salt,[8] which once are said to antedate the elements.[9] It is declared that man is made in the image of God, rather than of the

---

[1] *De ludo globi*, German transl. by F. Scharpff, *Des Nicolaus v. Cusa Wichtigste Schriften* (Freiburg i. Br., 1862), pp. 220–226.

[2] *Ibid.*, pp. 224–229.

[3] For this, Meyer (*op. cit.*, p. 54), has coined the word " Megistokosmos."

[4] Scharpff, *op. cit.*, pp. 229–230.

[5] *Ibid.*, pp. 247–8.

[6] *Ibid.*, p. 245. In another work, in an elaborate comparison of the State and an organic body, Nicholas declares that Christ is the heart; the church is Christ's body. Its soul, diffused and differentiated, is the priestly hierarchy.  Gierke, *op. cit.*, pp. 23–27, 132.

[7] *Interp. totius astron.*, in the Geneva folio edition of the works of Paracelsus (1658; copy in New York Public Library), vol. II, p. 664 a.  Unless otherwise noted, citations in this section refer to this edition.

[8] *De nat. rer.*, viii; vol. II, p. 101 b.

[9] *Phil. ad Ath.*, quot. by Erdmann, *op. cit.*, I, p. 619.

world,[1] but man's resemblance to the world comes in for a great deal of
emphasis. He is said to have been created from the "mass," [2] a handful
of the concentrated essence of the world,[3] and sometimes is regarded as
having been born from the universe.[4] The universe and man resemble
each other—heaven has the figure of a man, not, to be sure, corporeally,
but the figure of man himself.[5] Both the universe and man have the
same reason behind them; [6] each is self-governing; [7] heaven is essentially
a sphere, and man a globe; [8] the circle of heaven is like man's skin.[9]
Man's body contains the four elements in modified forms; [10] he desires
to eat because he is from the earth, to drink because he is from the water,
to breathe because he is from the air, and to be warm because he is from
the fire.[11] Again, man's body, like the universe, is composed of mercury,
sulphur, and salt.[12] Outside man, mercury becomes lightning; sulphur,
oil; and salt, alkali; [13] and, in the greater world, the ocean separates
Europe, Asia, and Africa, as a prefigured separation of the three principles.[14] The world is divided into sensible (corporeal) and insensible,
superior (sidereal) regions; the former is composed of mercury, sulphur,
and salt, the latter of mind and wisdom and knowledge.[15] From the
mass, two bodies, the sidereal and the elemental, are produced,[16] and man
contains a "magnet" from each.[17] Man's psychic powers are of sidereal
origin; [18] his imagination corresponds to the sun.[19] The result is that man
contains everything found in either sidereal or elemental regions [20]—

[1] *Interp. tot. astron.*; vol. II, p. 664 b.          [2] *Ibid.*, p. 664 a.

[3] *Explic. tot. astron.*; vol. II, p. 649 a.

[4] *De pestilitate*, tract. I; vol. I, p. 358.

[5] *De icteritiis seu morbis tinct.*, vol. I, p. 597 b.

[6] *Chirurg. mag.*, part IV (*De tumoris*), I, vi; vol. III, p. 105 b.

[7] *Paramirum*, tract. I, parenth. after ch. xiii; vol. I, p. 17 b.

[8] *De cutis apertionibus*, viii; vol. III, p. 63 b.

[9] *De colica* (first recens.); vol. I, p. 598 a.

[10] *Interp. tot. astron.*; vol. II, p. 664 b.

[11] *Paragranum*, tract. II; vol. I, p. 201 b.

[12] *Paramir. aliud.* (*De orig. morb. invis*); vol. I, p. 34 b.   *De colica* (second recens.);
vol. I, p. 631 b.

[13] *Chirurg. mag.*, part III, book III; vol. III, p. 86 b.

[14] *De nat. rer.*, book VIII; vol. II, p. 101 b.

[15] *Philosophia sagax*, book I, chap. 1; vol. II, p. 527 a.

[16] *Phil. sag.*, I, ii; vol. II, p. 533 a.

[17] *Ibid.*, p. 532, a, b.

[18] *Interp. tot. astron.*; vol. II, p. 665 b.

[19] *De virt. imaginat.*, iv; vol. II, p. 471 a.

[20] *Paramirum*, book IV; vol. I, p. 103 a and *passim*.

the characters of the four elements, fruits, metals, constellations, winds, trees, gems,[1] minerals,[2] sun, moon, planets, chaos, milky way, the two poles, and the zodiacal number; the universe of planets has in man its similar image and signature.[3] Man contains more than a thousand species of trees, minerals, manna, and metals,[4] and has the qualities of all animals.[5] Paracelsus employs a number of new phrases to character-ize man—he is "limbus minor," in which the universe of creatures exists;[6] "punctum cœli et terræ,"[7] "juvenile cœlum,"[8] "extractum totius machinæ mundi"[9] and "filius totius mundi."[9] The term "microcosmus" or its equivalent is used by Paracelsus more often than by any other writer—perhaps as much as by all the writers up to his time taken together. He was perhaps the originator of the term "macro-cosmus."

*2. Applications of Microcosmic Theories to Medicine.* The distinctive feature of the work of Paracelsus is his absurd attempt to turn the micro-cosmic theories to practical account in medicine. He uses them to ac-count for the origin of diseases and to indicate methods of treatment.[10] There is a pulse in the firmament, physiognomy in stars, chiromancy in minerals, spirits in winds, fevers in motions of the earth.[11] The stars have received from God the power of punishing men by inflicting diseases upon them.[12] Just as there are four elements, there are four chief kinds of diseases; diseases are produced in the body by salt, just as gems are produced in the earth by salt.[13] That which causes ulcers is found in each of the four elements.[14] A fever is an inner storm.[15] Just as the earth dries

---

[1] *De caus. morb. invis.*, III; vol. I, p. 124 a. This is an enumeration which Meyer (*op. cit.*, p. 61), neglecting Jewish and Arabian sources, calls the first detailed elucida-tion of the term microcosm.

[2] *Paramirum*, book IV; vol. I, p. 99 a.

[3] *Paragranum*, tract. II; vol. I, p. 197 b. *Paragran. alterius*, tract. II; vol. I, p. 236, a, b.

[4] *De causis et orig. luis gallicæ*, book V, chap. x; vol. III, p. 198 b.

[5] *De fund. sci. et sap.*, tract. III; vol. II, p. 517 a.

[6] *Duo alii lib. de podagricis morbis;* vol. I, p. 651 b.

[7] *Phil. sag.*, book I, chap. vii; vol. II, p. 567 b.

[8] *Paragran. alt.*, tract. II; vol. I, p. 236 a.

[9] *Phil. sag.*, I, ii; vol. II, pp. 532 b, 533 b.

[10] Cf. *Chirurg. mag.*, part IV, book IV, iii; vol. III, p. 119 b.

[11] *Paragran.*, I; vol. I, p. 191 b.

[12] *De pestilitate*, tract. II; vol. I, p. 380.

[13] *Chirurg. mag.*, part IV, book IV, ii; vol. III, p. 119 a.

[14] *Ibid.*, part III, book III; p. 86 a.

[15] Quot. by Erdmann, *op. cit.*, I, p. 621.

up, so the human body has varying rates of drying up; a parallel is drawn
between rain and food and drink—it is declared that man is sustained by
invisible rains.[1] There is a kind of cavity or emptiness in the world,
among the four elements, where man lives, and man has in his body a
corresponding cavity;[2] colic is due to wind which comes from the sidereal
region; there are four directions for colic, corresponding to the four
winds; the inner winds differ from the outer in that they can be moved by
external forces, and can cause pain.[3] There are as many kinds of planets,
stars, and pestilences as there are "virtues."[4] Paracelsus emphasizes
the bearing of the microcosmic theories upon diseases of the womb, saying
that such an emphasis will prevent mistakes.[5] The womb, separated
from the rest of the body as the body itself is from the external world, is
a world by itself—"mundus omnium minimus,"[6] "mundus minor,"
"mundus alter." The world is in a relation to man comparable to that of
man to the womb. Just as a fœtus lives in the firmament of the womb,
so man lives beneath the external firmament; and just as a microcosm
lies in the womb, so Adam lay in the womb of the four elements. Since
the womb is a world, its paroxysms resemble thunders, earthquakes, and
winds.[7] Paracelsus is not content with holding the microcosmic theory
himself; he is continually urging it upon the physicians. Since the
sidereal world and man are alike, and even inseparable and continuous,
surely a knowledge of astronomy will help the physician in diagnosis;[8] in
fact, a cure depends on it.[9] How can a physician hope to know man if
he does not know the world, the elements, the firmament?[10] He should
study the anatomy of external man—*i. e.*, the constitution of the universe—and learn anatomy from astronomy;[11] one thing is altogether to
be compared and explained by reference to another.[12] When it came to

---

[1] *De aridura*, second recens.; vol. I, pp. 625 b–626 a.

[2] *De colica*, first recens.; vol. I, p. 598 a.

[3] *De colica*, second recens.; vol. I, pp. 630 b–631 a.

[4] *De peste libri tres*, tract. III; vol. I, p. 428 a.

[5] *De caduco matricis*, II, iii; vol. I, p. 682 a.

[6] *Paramir.*, IV; vol. I, p. 86 a.

[7] *De caduc. matr.*, II, ii–vi; vol. I, pp. 678 a–688 b.

[8] *Ibid.*, I, ii; vol. I, p. 663 b.

[9] *De aridura*; vol. I, p. 626 a.

[10] *Paramir.*, IV; vol. I, p. 103 a.

[11] *Paragran.*, I; vol. I, p. 196 a—also *Modus pharmacandi*, tract. III; vol. I, p. 814 a, b.

[12] *De colica* (second recension); vol. I, p. 632 b.

remedies, Paracelsus believed in general that "like cures like," [1] through the release of natural forces.[2] Various metals,[3] and balsam,[4] he thought to have curative properties. Although many of his writings may be described as alchemical,[5] and he held various notions about panaceas, etc., which approximated those of the alchemists,[6] he was greatly interested in developing what would now be called specifics.[7]

*3. Place of Paracelsus in the History of Microcosmic Theories.* Paracelsus marks a transition stage in the history of microcosmic theories, exhibiting a unique combination of ancient and modern tendencies. In his reaction against blind allegiance to the works of older medical writers, he erected the theory that man is a microcosm into a position of central importance. But he attempted to hold and promulgate the theory in the face of, and even along with, what have since proved to be some of the chief forces which oppose it—namely, experimental methods. For Paracelsus, medicine is primarily an art, and an art proves itself, without needing experiments.[8] Experiments may sometimes extend the bounds of theory, but are often useless there; [9] Paracelsus attempts to found his methods rather upon great cosmic principles.[10] But as the world advanced farther into the modern period, such views were bound to be discredited; Paracelsus is roundly scored by Francis Bacon,[11] and his views are criticized even by J. B. van Helmont,[12] and Sir Thomas Browne.[13] Erdmann says that only since and by means of Paracelsus has the doctrine of the macrocosm and the microcosm been made the central point of the whole of philosophy.[14] But it must be noted that, except in the case of a

[1] *Cf. Paragranum*, I; vol. I, p. 196 b.

[2] *Cf.* Erdmann, *op. cit.*, I, p. 621.

[3] *Paramirum*, IV; vol. I, p. 99 a, b.

[4] *Archidoxorum*, X, iii; vol. II, p. 396.

[5] *Cf.* A. E. Waite, *The Hermetic and Alchemical Writings of Paracelsus* (2 vols., London, 1894).

[6] Erdmann, *op. cit.*, I, p. 622 f.

[7] See art., "Paracelsus," *Encyc. Brit.* (11), XX, p. 750.

[8] *De peste libri III*, exord.; vol. I, p. 413.

[9] *De ulceribus gall. X*, add.; vol. III, p. 142 b, 143 a.

[10] Erdmann, *op. cit.*, I, p. 623.

[11] *Advancement of Learning*, II (in *Works*, ed. B. Montagu, Philadelphia, 1846, vol. I, p. 202).

[12] *Inventio tartari, in morbis temeraria*, sec. 15 (in *Opera omnia*, 1707, p. 229).

[13] *Pseudodoxia epidemica*, II, iii (in *Works*, ed. Wilkin, London, 1852, vol. I, p. 140).

[14] *Op. cit.*, I, p. 613.

man like Valentine Weigel,[1] or Robert Fludd,[2] or others of the alchemists or occultists, the influence of Paracelsus was limited. His ideas were carried to such absurd extremes that, in all the more open fields of philosophy, they discredited rather than promoted the microcosmic theories. The fact that the theories were revived in later periods, for instance by Schelling and Fechner, is not to be traced to Paracelsus, so much as to other influences which we shall examine later.

### 4. GIORDANO BRUNO

*1. Bruno's Modifications of Older Views.* Students of Bruno have traced various differences between the Italian treatises of 1584 and the Latin poems of 1591,[3] but microcosmic theories run through both groups, often with slight modifications of older views. In the earlier group the Copernican system is extended from the sun and its planets to the whole universe,[4] which is regarded as an organism.[5] In the *Della causa* one of the interlocutors, the humanist Polyhimnio, appears with an atlas which, probably in allusion to the *De ludo globi* of Nicholas of Cusa, is said to contain the representation of a globe; in reply to a question, he affirms his belief in a correspondence between the parts of the macrocosm and those of the microcosm, but waives aside some fantastic deductions from

---

[1] Weigel (1533–1594), or whoever wrote the *Astrologia theologizata* attributed to him, held that both macrocosm and microcosm consisted of seven states or stages, each presided over by a planet (Eng. transl. by A. Kingsford, London, 1886, chap. VII, pp. 97–98). In the doctrines of man's creation and constitution there is close dependence upon Paracelsus (*Ibid.*, chap. II, esp. p. 76). The attempt is made to supplement the natural wisdom of astrology with the supernatural contribution of theology.

[2] Fludd (1574–1637) was the author of a work called *Utriusque cosmi maioris scilicet et minoris metaphysica physica atque technica historia.* (2 vols., Oppenheim, 1617). The title page has a curious drawing of man, the microcosm, within the circle of the macrocosm; man is represented as oriented with reference to the universe, his left side corresponding to the north (*Cf.* Lobeck, *op. cit.*, II, pp. 921, 924). The term macrocosm is used freely as a synonym for universe, and microcosm for man, both in this and in others of Fludd's works. His position is, in general, that of Paracelsus; he is also numbered among the Rosicrucians. In his *Tractatus theologo-philosophicus* (1617), he declares that man has a right to derive breath from the macrocosm, because of his kinship with the divine essence (book I, chap. vi, p. 26).

[3] *Cf.* Erdmann, *op. cit.*, I, pp. 657 ff., and *Encyc. Brit.* (11) IV, pp. 686–687.

[4] *Cena de la Ceneri*, quoted by W. Boulting, in *Giordano Bruno, His Life, Thought and Martyrdom* (London, 1916?), pp. 120–121.

[5] *Della causa, principio, ed uno*, dial. III (German transl. by P. Seliger, Leipzig, Reclam ed., p. 118).

such a view and changes the subject, before Theophilo, who is supposed to present Bruno's philosophy, has expressed an opinion.[1] Later on, Theophilo declares that man is no more like the infinite than is an ant, or a star, since all these things are without distinction as compared with the infinite.[2] But he also admits a comparison between the relations of the cosmic intellect to natural objects, on the one hand, and of our intellects to ideas, on the other hand.[3] At another point he indicates that there might be an interpretation of the world in accordance with the relations of numbers in the decimal notation.[4] In the *Del' infinito universo* Bruno writes that the course of nature is written in ourselves;[5] and rocks, lakes, rivers, springs, etc., he compares to various members or organs of the human body, adding that their accidents and disturbances, such as clouds, rain, snow, etc., are to be compared to human diseases.[6] Of the Latin poems, the *De immenso* contains the statement that everything is composed of the four elements, both we and all things found "maiori in corpore mundi."[7] There are processes of circulation in the universe, and in our bodies;[8] it is not necessary that the "blood" of the universe should be the same color as ours. The stars move themselves by their own internal principles, and move more freely even than we do.[9] There is a coition between sun and earth, resulting in the appearance of smaller living creatures.[10] But since the earth does not exhibit signs of actions and passions like ours, most men fail to see that the earth is our mother and progenitor, conserver, and moulder, from whose viscera we have our viscera and upon whose humours we are nourished.[11] In the *De monade, numero et figura*, it is said that just as the "megacosm" has one radiating sun, so the microcosm, man, has one heart.[12] This is the poem in which apparently all the things in heaven, earth, or imagination that could be

---

[1] *Della causa*, dial. III; Seliger transl., p. 97.

[2] *Ibid.*, dial. V; Seliger transl., p. 169. *Cf.* Bruno's *Cabala*, quoted by Boulting, *op. cit.*, p. 170.

[3] *Della causa*, dial. II; Seliger transl., pp. 70–71.

[4] *Ibid.*, dial. V; Seliger transl., pp. 192–193.

[5] Proem. epist., quoted by Boulting, *op. cit.*, p. 137.

[6] Cited by J. L. McIntyre, *Giordano Bruno* (London, 1903), p. 221, n.

[7] *De immenso et innumerabilibus*, V, ix (in *Opera latine conscripta*, ed. F. Tocco and H. Vitelli, Naples, etc., 1879–1891, vol. I (ii), p. 147).

[8] *Ibid.*, VI, viii; p. 185.

[9] *Ibid.*, V, xii; pp. 157–158.

[10] *Ibid.*, VI, i; p. 179.

[11] *Ibid.*, V, xii; p. 159.

[12] *De monade*, II; *Opera*, I (ii), p. 347.

associated with the numbers from 1 to 10 are mentioned and rather
loosely compared. Thus a connection is suggested between the four
elements, four winds, four beasts, four powers of mind, four kinds of
spirits,[1] with similar extravagances for the other numbers. It is notice-
able that among the nine senses to be used in interpreting sacred writings,
or the world about us, Bruno includes the "anagogicus," by which the
significance of one part of Scripture is made out by another part, and
analogies are detected between things.[2] All the things which are compared together make up the world, just as their characteristic numbers
lead up to the decad.[3]

2. *Bruno's Monadism.* The views just noted are not very original,
and would be of little importance except for two facts. They show that
one who adopted and even extended the Copernican system did not give
up his microcosmic views along with his geocentric; and they exhibit
some of the implications of Bruno's monadism. Bruno is supposed to
have taken some of the chief ideas for this from Nicholas of Cusa;[4] at
any rate, Bruno sees that there must be a limit or minimum of divisibility,
else there can be no substance,[5] and that there must be a unit or monad,
else there can be no number;[6] and the two are identified, since if either
were taken away, nothing would remain.[7] Three minima,[8] or irreduc-
ibles, are distinguished—God, the "Monas monadum,"[9] in whom both
greatest and least are one;[10] the soul, which serves as a center around
which the body is organized;[11] and the atom, which enters into the
composition of physical substances.[12] Besides these absolute monads,
there are relative monads or minima to be found almost everywhere.[13]
The result is a world in which "that which lies hidden in the small may
therefore be seen in the large, and that lies open in the whole which the
part everywhere conceals";[14] or, as he had already said in one of the

---

[1] *De monade*, V; pp. 385, ff.   [2] *Ibid.*, X; p. 456.   [3] *Ibid.*, XI; p. 459.
[4] *Cf.* Erdmann, *op. cit.*, I, p. 661; Boulting, *op. cit.*, p. 30.
[5] *De triplici minimo et mensura*, I, iii, 22; *Opera*, vol. I (iii), p. 141.
[6] *Ibid.*, I, ii, 13; p. 139.
[7] *Ibid.*, p. 140.
[8] Tocco, quoted by Boulting, *op. cit.*, p. 228.
[9] *De tripl. min.*, I, iv, schol.; vol. I (iii), p. 146.
[10] *Ibid.*, p. 147.
[11] *Ibid.*, I, iii, schol.; p. 143.
[12] *Ibid.*, I, ii, 29, ff.
[13] *Ibid.*, I, x; pp. 171 ff.
[14] *De immenso et innum.*, V, ix; *Opera*, vol. I (ii), p. 146.

Italian works, "in every man, in each individual, a world, a universe, regards itself." [1]  Thus a speculative monadism, which had perhaps begun to be hinted in the Italian treatises, was worked out in detail in the Latin poems.  The work of L. Stein has made plausible the view that Bruno's influence on Leibnitz has been overestimated; [2] but for Bruno, at least, the speculative monadism enabled the microcosmic theories to survive the shock of Copernicanism when that system was extended to include a universe regarded as infinite.

### 5. CAMPANELLA AND BOEHME

*1. Settings of the Microcosmic Theories of Campanella and Boehme.* From the point of view of microcosmic theories, Campanella and Boehme may be compared to show how the theories fitted different systems of theology during this period.  Campanella's theology is that of Thomas Aquinas, while Boehme is a Protestant mystic.  Campanella starts from a subjective standpoint and argues from the fact of thought to the existence of an infinite Being which excludes not-Being, but which, as God, produces the worlds from superfluity of love.[3]  Boehme seeks to formulate what he has felt concerning the reconciliation of evil and good in God who is the source of all existence, and from whom the world has evolved in seven complicated stages.[4]  Both men were involved in difficulties with ecclesiastical authorities, although not particularly on account of their microcosmic theories.

*2. Views of Campanella.*  Campanella thought that when man was compared with God, human science might well be called "micrology," [5] but, in order to advance his general argument by showing that nothing was without soul, he thought it legitimate to argue from inner experience to outer conditions.[6]  A corporeal spirit, he says, would not suffice to direct man; we find, in addition, an immortal soul.  How much more, therefore, must we conclude that the universe is governed by a world-soul.  If this were not so, then man, the "compendium epilogusque mundi," as certain theologians call him, would be superior to the world

---

[1] *Spaccio della bestia trionfante*, quot. by Boulting, *op. cit.*, p. 162.

[2] Stein, *Leibnitz und Spinoza* (Berlin, 1890), pp. 201–217.

[3] Erdmann, *op. cit.*, I, 643–646.

[4] G. W. Allen, art., Boehme, in Hastings, *Encyc. of Religion and Ethics*, vol. II, pp. 779, ff.

[5] Erdmann, *op. cit.*, I, p. 643.

[6] Campanella, *De sensu rerum*, II, xxxii (Frankfurt, 1620, p. 193).

itself. It is, declares Campanella, no argument against this view to say that worms, for instance, must then be "informed" with the world-soul; because there are parasites in and on the human body which do not share its reasoning power. The world has a spirit (heaven); a body (earth); and blood (the sea).[1] The argument from analogy is also used to show that just as our bodies abhor a vacuum, so must the world-body.[2] In another work it is said, again, that we are in a relation to the earth which is like that of the parasites of our body to us; and that the earth, in turn, is a large animal within a still larger one.[3] On a somewhat similar principle of extension from less to more inclusive units he describes an organization of human society.[4]

*3. Views of Boehme.* For Boehme, the world, which is the natural body of God,[5] is a living creature, like a man.[6] Man is a little world, having in himself the attributes of the great world—the sidereal, the elemental, and the divine.[7] Between macrocosm and microcosm there is unity and interaction.[8] Boehme elaborates in a fantastic and self-contradictory passage the doctrine of signatures—the whole body signifies heaven and earth; the body cavity (or, again, the bladder) signifies the space between the stars and the earth; the flesh (or, again, the lungs) signifies the element earth; the breath (or, the bladder) signifies the air; the heart signifies fire; and the blood (or, again, the liver) signifies water. The arteries signify the courses of the stars, and the intestines, their operation and wasting away. The sky is the heart of nature, like the brain in man's head.[9] Again, the sky, the stars, the depths of space between the stars, together with the earth, are compared to the Father; the sun, with its light and strength, to the Son; and the elements to the Holy Spirit.[10] Thus man is fundamentally akin to the universe which itself typifies the persons of the Trinity, and a basis is provided for man's reconciliation and mystical union with God.

---

[1] *Ibid.*, pp. 193–196.    [2] *Ibid.*, I, x; p. 38.

[3] See French transl., "*De l'univers et ses parties*," in L. Colet's edition of *Oeuvres choisis de Campanella* (Paris, 1844), p. 57.

[4] Erdmann, *op. cit.*, I, p. 649.

[5] *Aurora*, chap. ii (in Boehme's *Werke*, ed. by K. Schiebler, Leipzig, 1832, etc., vol. II, p. 28).

[6] *Vom Dreifachen Leben des Menschen*, VI, 48; *Werke*, vol. IV, p. 92.

[7] *Ibid.*, VI, 49; also Epistle 22, paragr. 7, *Werke*, vol. VII, p. 435; *Aurora*, ch. iii, *Werke*, vol. II, p. 41; *Signatura rerum*, I, 7, *Werke*, vol. III, p. 274.

[8] *Dreifach. Leben*, VI, 49.

[9] *Aurora*, chap. ii; *Werke*, vol. II, pp. 26–30.    [10] *Ibid.*, chap. III; pp. 36–38.

## 6. TREND FROM RATIONALISM TOWARD EMPIRICISM IN THIS PERIOD

*1. Microcosmic Theories of Writers less Important.* The trend away from the authoritarianism of the past and toward more empirical views of the world may be traced in most of the early modern writers hitherto considered; it is evident in general, too, when a number of other writers who either are less important, or who said less about the microcosmic theories, are grouped together. Thus L. Vives (1492–1540), who lived under the shadow of the realist and nominalist controversy,[1] but who was reaching out toward new methods, repeated the old view about the senses representing the four elements, and thought man could be called a little world because he was a complex of the strength and nature of all things.[2] J. Cardan (1501–1576), who was more rationalist than empiricist,[3] devoted a chapter of his *Arcana æternitatis* to a discussion of the likeness between the world and man.[4] John Dee, in his famous preface to the English edition of Euclid's *Elements* (1570), maintained that astronomy and cosmography, the sidereal and the terrestrial regions, could be correlated,[5] and that, since man is the microcosm for whom all creatures were created, the art of describing his perfect body should be called Anthropography, the Art of arts, which would combine a great number of contributions from other arts and sciences, from heaven and earth and all their creatures, into proof of "our Harmonious, and Microcosmicall constitution." According to Dee, Noah's ark and the Greek maxim, "Know thyself," were alike foretokens of the microcosmic theory.[6] The writings of Sir Thomas Browne exhibit some variations of attitude toward microcosmic theories. In the *Religio medici* (1642) he says that he thought that the theory that man is a microcosm was "only a pleasant trope of Rhetorick" until his "neer judgment" told him there was real truth therein, namely, that man combines the attributes of all species from the inorganic to the angelic.[7] But in his *Pseudodoxia epidemica* (1646), an indictment of popular superstitions, he declares that it is improbable that the body of man is magnetic; this, he says

---

[1] *Cf.* Windelband, *op. cit.*, p. 360.
[2] *De anima et vita*, I, 47 (Basle, 1538).
[3] Erdmann, *op. cit.*, I, p. 626.
[4] *Opera* (Lyons, 1663), vol. X, chap. VII.
[5] *Preface*, p. iii.
[6] *Ibid.*, p. ciiij.
[7] *Relig. med.* (Everyman ed., 1906), p. 39.

would "much advance the microcosmical conceit and commend the geography of Paracelsus."[1]   On the other hand, few books of any period have contained more "conceits" than Browne's *Garden of Cyrus* (1658), with its ransacking of the whole universe for examples of the "quincunx."[2] Another writer of the period is F. M. van Helmont (1618–1699) to whom, according to Stein,[3] Leibnitz owed his use of the term monad, rather than to Bruno.   Van Helmont speaks of "nobilissimam illam macrocosmi atque microcosmi analogiam," in a curious work with diagrams showing the human vocal apparatus in the form of the letters of the Hebrew alphabet.[4]  Stein quotes Leibnitz as mentioning a German translation, printed at Hamburg, of an English work by van Helmont, evidently entitled *Paradoxes of the Macrocosm and the Microcosm.*[5]  About this time a certain Martin Meyer published a worthless book, which ran at least to three editions, and in which the view that man is a microcosm was elaborated from previous sources by the aid of crude drawings and doggerel poetry in Latin and German.[6]

   *2. Decline of Microcosmic Views among the Great Scientists.*   The early modern writers whom we have thus far considered may be called, in general, adherents of the microcosmic theories.   The trend away from such views begins to be marked in the works of the great scientists. Even here there are sometimes isolated passages recalling the older views, but it is clear that empiricism and induction have made a great difference. The very first aphorism of Bacon's *Novum Organum* lays down the principle that

> "Man, as the minister and interpreter of nature, does and under-
> stands as much as his observations on the order of nature, either
> with regard to things or the mind, permit him, and neither knows nor
> is capable of more."

It is not surprising, then, to find Bacon criticizing the fantastic theories

---

[1] *Pseudod. epidem.*, II, iii (in *Works*, ed. Wilkin, London, 1852, vol. I, p. 140).

[2] *Cf. Encyc. Brit.* (11), vol. IV, pp. 666–667.

[3] *Leibnitz und Spinoza*, pp. 201–217.

[4] *Alphabeti vere naturalis Hebraici brevissima delineatio* (Sulzbach, 1657 or 1667), esp., p. 37.

[5] Stein, *op. cit.*, p. 213, n. 1, referring to Leibnitz; *Otium Hanov.*, p. 226 (Dutens, VI, 331).  *Cf.* H. Ritter, *Gesch. der Phil.*, vol. XII (Heidelberg, 1853), p. 7, n. 1; pp. 33, 34.

[6] *Homo microcosmus . . macrocosmo expositus* (3d ed., Frankfurt, 1670); copy in New York Public Library.

of Paracelsus,[1] and saying that the alchemists have taken the term microcosm in a sense too gross and literal, and have spoiled the elegance and distorted the meaning of it.[2] And still there are traces of microcosmic theories in Bacon. If we look to final causes, man may be regarded as the center of the world. If man were taken away from the world, the rest would seem to be all astray, without aim or purpose; whereas all things seem to be going about man's business and not their own. Bacon could even find some meaning in the old theories of man's composition; for, after all, the body of man is of all existing things both the most mixed and the most organic,[3] and, directly or indirectly, it is nourished by all things.[4] Throughout the great bulk of Bacon's writing, however, it is clear that man is the end rather than the imitation of the universe, and that the microcosmic theories are illustrative rather than essential. They played a rather more important part in the work of Kepler, who, in his *De harmonice mundi*, presents his third law in a setting which suggests that he may have been led to it by doctrines as old as Pythagoreanism. He regarded the earth as a great animal whose breathing depended upon the sun, and whose sleeping and waking caused the rise and fall of the oceans.[5] Newton closed his *Principia* with an allusion to a cosmic spirit pervading all bodies and exciting sensation and volition in animals by its vibrations—

> "but these are things which can not be explained in few words, nor are we furnished with that sufficiency of experiments which is required to an accurate determination and demonstration of the laws by which this electric and elastic spirit operates." [6]

Robert Boyle dissents from the theory of Paracelsus, explicitly on the ground that man was made not in the world's image, but in God's; [7] but implicit throughout Boyle's writings is the view that the universe is to be studied by the "Christian virtuoso" with the aid of experimental methods.

---

[1] *Adv. of Learning*, II; *Works*, ed. Montagu, I, 202. *Cf. De augmentis scientiarum*, IV, ii, and *Sylva sylvarum*, cent. X, i.

[2] *De sapientia veterum*, xxvi.

[3] *De sap. vet., loc. cit.*    [4] *Adv. of Learning*, II; Montagu I, 202.

[5] *Cf.* Fechner, *Zend-Avesta* (1854), vol. I, p. 61, n., and A. M. Clerke, in *Encyc. Brit.* (11), XV, 750. Kepler took pains to state some of the points at which his mathematical theories of harmony differed from the fancies of Robert Fludd. *De harm.*, V, appendix; *Opera* (ed. C. Frisch, Frankfurt, 1864, vol. V, pp. 331, ff.).

[6] *Principia*, book III, schol.

[7] *Usefulness of Philosophy* (Oxford, 1663), p. 100.

## 7. THE MICROCOSMIC THEORY OR METAPHOR OF HOBBES

*1. The Conception of the State as a Leviathan.* Along with the writers
of this period of changing conceptions concerning the microcosmic
theories should be mentioned Thomas Hobbes, whose *Leviathan*, even if
he himself did not mean the conception to be taken literally, may be
viewed as a prototype of more definite and literal organismic theories.
For Hobbes, the commonwealth is "but an artificial man, though of
greater stature and strength than the natural." [1]   In this commonwealth,
the sovereignty is an artificial soul, which gives life and motion to the
whole body.   The magistrates and other officers are artificial joints; or,
again, organs of will.[2]   Reward and punishment are the nerves, by
which every joint and member, fastened to the seat of sovereignty, is
made to perform his duty; or, again, the financial channels are the nerves
and arteries.[3]   "The nutrition of a commonwealth consisteth in the plenty
and distribution of materials conducing to life; in concoction or preparation; and, when concocted, in the conveyance of it by convenient con-
duits to the public use." [4]   The wealth and riches of the particular
members are the strength of the commonwealth; or, again, money is its
blood.[5]   The people's safety is the business of the commonwealth,
counsellors are its memory, equity and laws are its artificial reason and
will, concord is its health, sedition its sickness, and civil war its death.
Colonies are the children of the commonwealth.[6]   Among the "diseases"
of a commonwealth analogues are found for hydrophobia, epilepsy, and
ague.[7]   In the *De corpore politico*, invasion is compared to the violent
death of a commonwealth, while sedition is the death of a commonwealth
"like to that which happeneth to a man from sickness and distemper." [8]
The parallel is carried even into the theory of a successful revolution,
which must present one body of rebellion in which the intelligence is the
life, number the limbs, weapons the strength, and a directing head, the
unity.[9]

[1] *Leviathan* (*Works*, ed. W. Molesworth, London, 1839, vol. III, pp. ix, x).   This
reference covers statements in this paragraph, except as otherwise noted.

[2] *Ibid.*, p. 230.

[3] *Ibid.*, pp. 238–239.

[4] *Ibid.*, p. 232.

[5] *Ibid.*, pp. 238–239.

[6] *Ibid.*, pp. 239–240.

[7] *Ibid.*, pp. 315–320.

[8] *De corp. polit.*, chap. VIII; *Works*, vol. IV, p. 200.

[9] *Ibid.*, p. 209.

*2. Function of Microcosmic Views for Hobbes.*   Such an organismic or quasi-organismic theory as this enabled Hobbes to present the state as a closely-knit and powerful creation, and at the same time to recognize the importance of individuals within it.   He is at once authoritarian and individualistic.   Such organismic or quasi-organismic bonds between individuals strengthen his conception of a convention or contract, whether the latter be alleged as a historical fact, or pictured for its moral effect.   But whether Hobbes is to be called an organicist, or his conception of a Leviathan is to be regarded as a metaphor, depends upon one's definitions of these terms.   Hobbes is not as insistent upon literal interpretation as are some of the later organicists—once he calls the body politic a fictitious body; [1] but on the other hand he must attach a certain seriousness to it in order to picture the individual as contained within the binding relationships of the state.

8. Summary: Microcosmic Theories in the Early Modern Period

The microcosmic theories undergo numerous modifications in their early modern restatements, and exhibit traces of the ferment observable throughout the world of thought.   They are common to both peripatetics and their opponents and are found among both Catholics and Protestants. Judging from the prevalence of microcosmic theories, it would have to be said that the rise of the Copernican astronomy did not lessen the importance which man ascribed to himself; rather, it was by the aid of microcosmic theories that man's estimate of himself kept abreast of the expanding universe.   But the beginning of a decided trend away from the theories, which has persisted to our own day, may be noted in the empiricism of the great scientists.   The tendency begins to appear to regard the older microcosmic views as illustrative metaphors rather than as philosophical doctrines.

Appendix I—Microcosmic Theories and Alchemy in the Early Modern Period

Some of the writers on alchemy who were important in the general field of philosophy have been mentioned; but something should be said of alchemy in general, and of some early modern writers who were more obscure but not less ardent in their views on the microcosmic theories. Though subjected to wide variations, the central idea of alchemy was

[1] *De corp. polit.*, chap. VIII; *Works*, vol. IV, p. 140.

that since all substances were composed of one "prima materia" they could by appropriate means be first reduced to this, and then developed from this into other forms.   To this "prima materia" the name Mercury (not ordinary mercury, but the "mercury of the philosophers") was assigned.   When this had been obtained, it was to be treated with "Sulphur" to confer upon it the desired qualities.   This Sulphur, or a preparation from it, was called the elixir, or the philosophers' stone. (See H. M. Ross, article "Alchemy," in *Encyc. Brit.* (11) vol. I, p. 520). Since it was supposed to contain the essence of all substances, it was known as the microcosm (E. A. Hitchcock, *Remarks upon Alchemy and the Alchemists*, Boston, 1857, p. 40).   Its preparation was linked with astrological lore, on the principle that things in the earth should correspond to things in heaven.   Many of the writers employ the notion of a magnet in man, and in the world (Hitchcock, *op. cit.*, p. 93).   Under philosophical influences the concepts became further involved; the "prima materia" became known as the soul of the metal, and the philosophers' stone as a curative agent which could "make the sick metal well" (H. Silberer, *Problems of Mysticism and its Symbolism*, transl. by Jelliffe, N. Y., 1917, p. 114).    On the other hand, the philosophers' stone came to have moral influence attributed to it; just as it ennobled the metals, so it could ennoble man (L. Figurier, *L'alchimie et les alchimistes*, Paris, 1860, p. 21).   The stone was regarded as an image of the Trinity; as it was composed of mercury, sulphur, and salt, so man was composed of spirit, soul, and body (Hitchcock, *op. cit.*, pp. 94, 136; Silberer, *op. cit.*, p. 154).   The soul of man is called a "microcosmic heaven" (Silberer, p. 81).

According to J. Grashofer's *Aperta arca.* . . . (Frankfurt, 1623, Vorrede, p. 7) the term "microcosm" was apparently used in the title of a book by F. Tidicaeus.   Among the alchemists who elaborated these ideas with mention of microcosmic theories were (1) Thomas Norton (d. 1477), author of *The Ordinal of Alchemy* (in the *Hermetic Museum*, Eng. transl., ed. A. E. Waite, London, 1893, vol. II; see esp. p. 64); (2) George Ripley (d. 1490), author of *The All Wise Doorkeeper* (Hermetic Museum, II; see esp. p. 319, and *cf.* Hitchcock, p. 38): (3) J. Frizius, author of the *Summum bonum, verum . . . alchymiæ . . . subjectum* (Frankfurt, 1629; see Silberer, *op. cit.*, pp. 177 ff.): (4) A. van Suchten (see Benedictus Figulus, *A Golden Casket of Nature's Marvels*, publ. at Strasbourg in 1608, Eng. transl., London, 1893, by J. Elliott, pp. 22–23).

Among those who wrote on the microcosmic theory in the more general sense, and made more or less distinctive contributions to it, were (1) Alipili, author of *Centrum naturæ concentratum* (see Hitchcock, p. 35, and Silberer, p. 153): (2) M. Sendivogius (d. about 1604) who published the *Novum lumen chemicum* (Hermetic Museum, II; *cf.* I, p. xi, and see esp. II, pp. 87–88) and *De sulphure* (*Ibid.*, see esp. pp. 138–139): (3) M. Meyer (1568–1622), author of *A Subtle Allegory concerning the Secrets of Alchemy* (in *Hermetic Museum*, II; see esp. pp. 206 ff.): (4) B. Figulus, author of the *Golden and Blessed Casket*, cited above: (5) M. Ruland (*Lexicon alchemiæ*, Frankfurt, 1612, esp. p. 335): and (6) J. Walchius, author of a commentary on J. Grashofer's *Kleine Bauer* (Strasbourg, 1619; see esp. p. 118). For references on alchemist writings during the 18th century see *A. B. C. vom Stein der Weisen*, in *Geheime Wissenschaften*, ed. by A. von d. Linden, Berlin, 1915, vols. V, VI, VII, VIII; esp. vol. VIII, pp. 71, 127–128, 167–198. Most of the works here cited are in the New York Public Library.

APPENDIX II—USE OF THE TERM "MICROCOSM" TO DENOTE MAN, IN ENGLISH LITERATURE FROM 1400 TO 1650

In connection with the philosophical theories, it is significant that during the early modern period the term "microcosm" or its equivalent was used in English literature as a synonym for man. Several instances of this are noted in the *New English Dictionary*, under "microcosm." Besides the references there given may be noted J. Lydgate, *The Assembly of Gods* (1403 or 1412); ed. O. L. Triggs, in *Univ. of Chicago English Studies*, vol. I (1895), lines 932 (see Triggs's note, p. 102), 995, 1250, etc., *passim*. There are additional references in Lydgate, *De Guil. Pilgr.*, ed. F. J. Furnivall, *Early English Text Society*, extra series 83, London, 1901, part II, lines 21168–21173, 21233. Interesting in this connection because of its long pedigree and possible affiliations is Lydgate's translation of the *Secrees of Old Philisoffres*, ed. by R. Steele, *Early Eng. Text Soc.*, extra series 66, London, 1894, lines 2291 ff. (*cf.* Introd., p. xv). The term is used by Philip Stubbs, *Anatomie of Abuses* (1583), p. iii; by Joshua Sylvester, *The Divine Weeks*, ed. T. W. Haight, Waukesha, 1908, lines 327 ff., and by Sir John Davies, *Nosce te ipsum* (1599)— see A. B. Grosart, ed., *Complete Poems of Sir J. D.*, in the *Fuller Worthies Library*, London, 1869, pp. 47, 55, 97 ff. Grosart, p. 98, n., says that the word "microcosm" is found "in theological (Puritan) writings." John Davies of Hereford published a long poem entitled *Microcosmos, The*

*Discovery of the Little World, with the Government Thereof* (1603); see his *Complete Works*, ed. by A. B. Grosart, Edinburgh, 1878, esp. I, c, p. 85, col. 2, line 16. In Shakespeare's *Coriolanus*, Menenius, after describing his own character, says "If you see this in the map of my microcosm, follows it that I am known well enough, too?" (II, i, 68). The idea that man is a microcosm controls Phineas Fletcher's hideous *Purple Island* (1633); see H. Headley's ed., London, 1816, esp. Canto I, xli, xlvi, and V, viii. The term was used again as a title by Thomas Nabbes in his *Microcosmus, a Morall Maske* (1637); ed. by A. H. Bullen in *Old English Plays*, new series, vol. II, London, 1887; see esp. p. 174. P. Heylin, J. Earle, and Joshua Sylvester used the term "microcosm," or "microcosmography" to denote small portions of the world or brief descriptions of them.

# CHAPTER IV

## MICROCOSMIC THEORIES IN PHILOSOPHY FROM DESCARTES TO SPENCER

### 1. The Span of this Chapter

In spite of the fact that some of the men already considered as having belonged to the transition period were in point of time his contemporaries, one may make an epochal division in the history of philosophy at the time when the great mind of Descartes grappled with world problems. Descartes was apparently not interested in microcosmic theories; his initial attitude of doubt made him begin by underestimating the external world, and the philosophy of substance at which he arrived was reached by divesting the external world of everything which might make its resemblance to man interesting. But the abstract metaphysics of Descartes was a forerunner of the abstract metaphysics of Spinoza, and his emphasis upon the subjective turned men's thoughts in the direction in which they were later developed, and involved in problems of epistemology, from the time of Locke to that of Fichte and Schopenhauer. The tendencies which derived encouragement from Descartes might, if unchecked, have excluded from philosophy even the few resemblances between the universe and man which the growing empiricism of the age could countenance; but they were not allowed to develop unchecked. Leibnitz formulated a more concrete metaphysics, and Hegel and Schelling and their followers opposed subjectivism when it reached extremes. Even empiricism was not left in undisputed possession of the field; Fechner went beyond it by methods of speculation, while Lotze met its mechanistic features with a philosophy of values. Finally Spencer assembled the empirical data around a concept of evolution, citing some famous illustrations which, with only slight changes of presupposition or interest, might have served as data for microcosmic theories.

### 2. The Metaphysical Systems of Spinoza and Leibnitz

*1. The Pantheism of Spinoza.* One might expect that the pantheism of Spinoza, like that of the Stoics, would combine with some microcosmic theory;[1] but one finds Spinoza's argument passing by on either side of such views. On the one hand, he emphasizes the infinite differences between man and the world. On the other hand, the resemblances which he notes are exceedingly abstract;[2] when viewed "sub specie æternitatis" the individuality which, for a microcosmic theory, would be compared to the universe is absorbed into it.

*2. The Monadism of Leibnitz.* Spinoza pictures the universe as a composite individual; Leibnitz thinks of it as an aggregate of individual monads. The similarities between various portions of the universe which any monadism is able to exhibit are in the case of Leibnitz heightened by a parallelistic psychology and the doctrine of preëstablished harmony,[3] as well as by his recognition of the method of analogy.[4] For Leibnitz, there is a world of creatures, of living beings, of entelechies, of souls, in the smallest particle of matter; each portion of matter "may be conceived as a garden full of plants and as a pond full of fishes." But each branch of the plant, each member of the animal, is also such a garden, or such a pond.[5] Each monad, in spite of the fact that it "has no windows," is in ideal relations with every other; hence every such simple substance carries with it the impress of all other things, and appears as a living and everlasting mirror of the universe,[6] although it must be made clear that a monad is by no means equivalent to the universe which it represents.[7] Monads may be grouped in compound substances or bodies; each important monad is the center of such a substance. In these compounds, some monads dominate over others; they may be organized for feeling and memory.[8] A monad joined with a soul makes a living creature, an animal; because the monad reflects the order of all things, the animal's body becomes an organism, and the soul becomes an organized individuality.[9] In the "little world" the circulation of the blood has been discovered, and in the "great world" the motion of the stars.[10]

---

[1] *Cf.* Weber, *History of Philosophy* (transl. Thilly), p. 334.

[2] *Ethics*, II, xiii, lemma 7, n. *Cf.* the 15th letter, quoted by E. Caird, art. " Cartesianism," *Encyc. Brit.* (11), V, 422–423.

[3] *Monadology*, 78.

[4] *Cf.* H. Höffding, *History of Modern Philosophy*, Eng. transl. by R. Meyer (London, 1908), vol. I, p. 348.

[5] *Monadology*, 66. *Cf. Ibid.*, 70.       [6] *Ibid.*, 56.       [7] *Ibid.*, 60.

[8] *Principes de la nature et de la grace* (in *Philosoph. Schriften*, ed. C. Gerhardt, Berlin, 1887, vol. VI, p. 599).

[9] *Monadology*, 63, 64.

[10] Correspondence, in Stein, *Leibnitz und Spinoza*, pp. 333–334.

Each soul pictures the universe from its own point of view; it is as if God had varied the universe as many times as there are souls. Each soul is "comme un univers concentré." [1] Between body and soul a preëstablished harmony is possible because they both are representations of the same universe.[2] We must not think that true unity or substance is confined to man alone,[3] but, since the soul is representative in a very exact manner of the universe, the series of representations which the soul will produce for itself will naturally correspond to the series in the universe.[4] Our soul is architectonic in its voluntary actions, and, discovering the science according to which God has regulated things, it imitates in its development and in its little world, where it is permitted to exercise itself, what God does in the large world.[5] Once it is said that our souls, like little gods, make worlds; [6] again, there is a distinction between souls, which represent only the created world, and spirits which are, in addition, images of God, and each in its circle a little divinity.[7] Every spirit, being, like a separate world, sufficient to itself, independent of every other creature, involving the infinite, expressing the absolute, is as durable, as stable, and as absolute, as the universe of creatures itself.[8] By Leibnitz's expositions [9] of these views, microcosmic theories won an established place in speculative metaphysics, although accounts with subjectivism and empiricism were still to be settled.

## 3. THE CRITICAL PHILOSOPHY: FROM LOCKE TO FICHTE

*1. Decline of Interest in Microcosmic Theories.* Interest in resemblances between the universe and man was presently lost in the all-engrossing critical problem. As the questions raised by Locke passed through the hands of Berkeley, Hume, Kant, and Fichte, the outer world was reduced to a status more and more subordinate, until it came to be of little importance whether man resembled it or not. Here and

---

[1] Letter, Gerhardt, vol. III, pp. 347–348. *Cf. Philosoph. Abhandl.*, in *Ibid.*, vol. IV, p. 434.

[2] *Monadology*, 78.

[3] Letter to Arnauld; *Schriften*, Gerhardt, vol. II, p. 98.

[4] *New System of Nature*, in *Philosophical Works*. Eng. transl. by Duncan (New Haven 1908), p. 85.

[5] *Theodicy*, in Duncan, *op. cit.*, p. 305.

[6] Corresp., in Stein, *op. cit.*, p. 333.

[7] *Monadology*, 83.

[8] *New System of Nature;* Duncan, *op. cit.*, p. 85.

[9] *Cf. Encyc. Brit.* (11), art., "Microcosm."

there terms once used in the development of microcosmic theories were used with new or at least with restricted connotations—as when Locke used the terms "little world of man's own understanding" and "great world of visible things," [1] and Kant used the words "macrocosmically" and "microcosmically," meaning by them the infinitely great and the infinitely small limits of the "mathematically unconditioned" at which his "regressus" is said to aim.[2] Some of the views of these men might easily be construed in microcosmic terms—as when Hume hints at a comparison of the process of association of ideas to that of attraction in physics,[3] and Kant declares that pure speculative reason is so constituted that it forms a true organism,[4] and Fichte says that nature in general forms an organic whole, and is posited as such [5]—but it is easy to see that the weight of their interest is not upon such a comparison. Everything is rendered in terms of psychology and epistemology.[6] Reid, with his opposition to subjectivism, could write that it was not without reason that man had been called an epitome of the universe, since he had something in common with inanimate things, with vegetables, animals, and rose at last to the rational life;[7] but this isolated passage seems more like an illustration drawn from the ancient view than a piece of fresh reasoning developed in this period.

2. *Microcosmic Theories Stated in Hume's Dialogues.* The most important recognition which microcosmic theories received during this period was when Hume, in his *Dialogues Concerning Natural Religion*, made one of his characters, Philo, present a restatement of ancient views concerning analogies between an organism and the universe, in opposition to the argument, as presented by Cleanthes, that the constitution of the universe affords evidence of a designer. Philo is represented as saying that the little agitation of the brain called thought ought not to be made the model for the whole universe,[8] *i.e.*, that purposiveness ought not to be

---

[1] *Essay Concerning Human Understanding*, I, ii.

[2] *Critique of Pure Reason*, Div. II, Book II, chap. ii, sec. 2 (Eng. transl. by M. Müller, London, 1881, vol. II, p. 363).

[3] *Treatise of Human Nature*, Book I, Part I, sec. iv (ed. T. H. Green and T. H. Grose, London, 1886, vol. I, p. 321).

[4] Preface to second edition of *Critique of Pure Reason*: Müller, *op. cit.*, vol. I, p. 385.

[5] *Science of Right*, Eng. transl., by A. Kroeger (London, 1907), p. 119.

[6] A later example is found in Sir W. Hamilton's *Discourses on Philosophy and Literature* (London, 1852), p. 9.

[7] *Essays on the Active Powers of Man*, III, I, i (London, 1827, p. 487).

[8] *Dialogues* (edition of 1779), II, p. 477.

projected into the universe. A mental world requires a cause as much as a material; we have specimens in miniature of both of them, for our mind resembles the one, and a vegetable or animal body resembles the other.[1] In fact, the universe resembles an animal or organized body, and seems to be actuated with a similar principle of life and motion, and to exhibit similar processes of circulation, repair of waste, and coöperation of parts—so that one may infer that the universe is an animal, and that God is its soul.[2] To this Cleanthes is made to rejoin that the analogy is defective in many circumstances; there are in the universe no organs of sense, no seat of thought or reason, no precise origin of motion or of action; the universe, in short, seems to resemble a vegetable more than an animal.[3] Philo on his part develops the latter analogy by the statement that the universe, like a tree, produces seeds, which, being scattered into the surrounding chaos, vegetate into new worlds. A comet is the seed of a world; after it has been fully ripened, by passing from star to star, it is tossed into the unformed elements which everywhere surround the universe, and sprouts up into a new system. Or, if the world be considered as an animal, a comet is the egg of that animal, and its development is like the hatching of an ostrich's egg in the sand.[4] If we are to get a cosmogony, we may say that the world is more similar to a process of generation than of fabrication.[5] In the closing words of the *Dialogues* the views of Cleanthes are given preference to those of Philo, so that it is hard to tell what weight Hume intended to attach to the latter. At any rate, we have a statement of microcosmic views in a time when they were not prevalent, whether or not Hume "inclines toward an organic conception of the universe." [6]

## 4. THE FRENCH ENLIGHTENMENT: ROUSSEAU

*1. Evidences of Decline of Microcosmic Views in France.* The philosophers of the French Enlightenment resemble the English philosophers of the period in that little attention is paid to the older microcosmic theories. Diderot's great *Encyclopédie* criticized the notion that man is an abridgment of the universe on the ground that man must then sum up not

---

[1] *Dialogues*, IV, p. 491.
[2] *Ibid.*, VI, pp. 503–504.
[3] *Ibid.*, VI, p. 506; *cf.* VII, p. 510.
[4] *Ibid.*, VII, p. 511.
[5] *Ibid.*, VII, p. 512.
[6] F. Thilly, *Hist. of Philos.* (New York, 1914), p. 361.

merely the good of the universe but also its evil, and stated that the word "microcosme" was obsolete.[1] But the whole work was conceived humanistically if not microcosmically; it was proposed to "introduce man into our work as he is placed in the universe, a common center," and to look among the principal faculties of man for the general division adopted in the work.[2] For Holbach, man is a production of nature, partially resembling it and partially subject to its laws, but differing somewhat from it and subject to laws determined by the diversity of his conformation. Man's existence is coördinated with that of the earth; but man has no right to think of himself as privileged in comparison with the rest of nature.[3]

2. *Rousseau's Theory of Society.* While there was thus no inclination in this period toward microcosmic theories in the physical sense, Rousseau, by some quasi-metaphorical statements in *Le contrat social*, kept the way open for a later development of microcosmic theories in the social sense—*i. e.*, of organismic theories of society. Rousseau maintained that the social contract produced a moral and collective body, a "personne publique."[4] As nature gives to every man absolute power over his members, so the social pact gives to the political body similar power over its members.[5] For nations, as for men, there are times of youth and maturity;[6] limits of advantageous size;[7] disease, and death.[8] The government is, on a small scale, what the whole body politic is on a large scale. The coöperation of mental and physical forces in man's action is paralleled by the coöperation of the legislative and executive power in a state; just as the former requires centralization, so does the latter.[9] The legislative power is the heart of the state, the executive power is the brain. Just as a man might live even though his brain were paralyzed, but must succumb if his heart stops, so the state might survive a lapse of executive power, but not of legislative power.[10]

5. REACTIONS FROM SUBJECTIVISM: FROM HERDER TO SCHOPENHAUER.

*1. Herder's Philosophy of History.* After subjectivism had gone to extremes in the work of Fichte, other German thinkers led a reaction against it; and as soon as this reaction set in, it led to different estimates

---

[1] *Encyclopédie* (Geneva, 1778) vol., XXI, p. 820.
[2] Art., "Encyclopédie," *ibid*, vol. XII, pp. 382-383.
[3] *Système de la nature*, I, vi (London, 1770, pp. 79, 84, 88).
[4] *Le contrat social*, I, vi.    [5] *Ibid.*, II, iv.    [6] II, viii.
[7] II, ix.    [8] III, xi.    [9] III, i.    [10] III, xi.

of the microcosmic theories.  Thus, while Kant's anthropology opposed free human development to nature, Herder, in his *Ideen zur Philosophie der Geschichte der Menschheit*, urged that human history be viewed in its astronomical, geological, and biological setting.  According to Herder it was after many vicissitudes among the lower forms of life that the crown of the earth's organization, man, appeared—the microcosm. Man is the son of all the elements and natures; he is their "erlesenster Inbegriff." [1]  In the course of development, the various species show more and more organization as they approach man, as though they were tending toward him; but Herder would avoid all fantastic systems, in which plants and rocks are thought of as external members of man's body— such imaginings only obscure the real resemblances between the species. [2] The study of man's capacities leads to the view that man is the connecting link between two worlds, the natural and the spiritual; in man, nature passes from the one to the other. [3]  Human history is regarded as having passed from a period of infancy, in the oriental civilizations, to its old age, in Christianity. [4]  So far as his microcosmic theories are concerned, Herder is not very original, but his work, coming at the time when it did, was very influential.

2. *The Microcosmic Theories of Schelling*.  In the heat of his revolt against the Fichtean view of nature as a postulate of the Ego, Schelling put forth one after another the various confusing formulations of his philosophy of nature. [5]  Without attempting to discuss the details of the differences between them, one may note, in general, that he held that a common principle binds organic and inorganic processes; [6] this principle, which makes of nature one great organism, [7] is identified with the world-

---

[1] *Ideen zur Philos. der Gesch. der Menschheit*, I, chap. iii.

[2] *Ibid.*, II, chap. iv (4).

[3] *Ibid.*, V, chap. vi.

[4] *Cf.* R. Falckenberg, *History of Modern Philosophy* (transl. Armstrong, N. Y., 1893), p. 311.

[5] The works of chief importance in this connection are the *Ideen zu einer Philosophie der Natur* (1797); *Von der Weltseele* . . . (1798); *Erster Entwurf eines Systems der Naturphilosophie* (1799); *Einleitung zu dem Entwurf* . . . (1799); *Allgemeine Deduktion des Dynamischen Processes* . . . (1800); *System der Gesammten Philosophie und der Naturphilosophie insbesondere* (1804).  These are all to be found in the *Sämmtliche Werke*, edited by Schelling's sons (Stuttgart and Augsburg, 1856, etc.).  They are cited here by the words *Ideen, Weltseele, Entwurf, Einleitung, Deduktion*, and *System*, respectively, and by reference to volume and page of the collected works.  All the volumes here cited belong in the first series of that edition.

[6] *Weltseele*, II, 347; also, *Ibid.*, II, 350.          [7] *Ibid.*, II, 569.

soul of the ancients.[1]  He held, further, that nature develops in analogy with reason.[2]  In order to describe this development he brought from subjectivism the duality of concepts emphasized in the Kantian antinomies and in the Fichtean doctrine of thesis, antithesis, and synthesis.[3] In the pure productivity of nature nothing can be distinguished except under the condition of duality; but productivity, thus limited, gradually materializes itself and acquires forms, more and more fixed, which constitute an evolutionary series (dynamische Stufenfolge) in nature.[4] The world of nature develops through three cycles (Potenzen), which may be called those of homogeneous matter, qualitatively differentiated matter, and organic processes.[5]  In the first of these cycles, the universe is initially organized in a gravitation system,[6] in which things may be said to be outwardly one.[7]  This gravitation principle is opposed, in the same cycle, by the light principle (das Lichtwesen—not ordinary light, but something more like the world-soul), in which things may be said to be in inner union.[8]  The two principles are, however, essentially one, and in their identity there is manifested the "Band," or copula, which synthesizes all dualities.[9]  Out of this essential oneness is produced a second cycle, or Potenz, also triadic, consisting of magnetism, electricity, and chemical processes.[10]  In this portion of his system, Schelling approaches Leibnitz when he declares that every part of matter is a copy of the whole universe.[11]  The light principle by imparting rest to movement makes a thing a mirror of the All.[12]  In every product the infinite productivity of nature is concentrated; in every product there is the germ of a universe.[13]  Individual things are related as organs of the All.[14]  The third cycle, that of organic nature, is only a higher power of the inorganic; and the principle of construction of all living forms is found in opposition of direction.[15]  Where the typical process of synthesis of opposed factors asserts itself in individuals, there is "Mikrokosmus, Organismus," a completed exposition of the general life of substance in a special life, a world in miniature.[16]  Animation is a building of the Whole into an individual.[17]  An organism is not homogeneous, but is like the

[1] *Weltseele;* II, 381, 569.        [2] *Einleitung;* III, 273-274.
[3] *Ibid.,* III, 317.  Cf. *Ibid.,* III, 299.        [4] *Ibid.,* III, 297-302.
[5] See Falckenberg, *Hist. of Mod. Philos.,* p. 452.
[6] *Einleitung;* III, 312.        [7] *Weltseele;* II, 369.        [8] *Ibid.,* II, 368-9.
[9] *Ibid.,* II, 370, ff.        [10] *Ibid.,* II, 373.        [11] *Ibid.,* II, 359.        [12] *Ibid.,* II, 370.
[13] *Einleitung;* III, 290-291.        [14] *System;* VI, 431.        [15] *Einleitung;* III, 304.
[16] *Weltseele;* II, 374.        [17] *Ibid.,* II, 364.

universe, a totality, a system of things.[1] It is said that in this cycle the principle of gravitation reappears in the plants, and in the female sex, and that of light reappears in the animals, and in the male sex, and the principle of the "Band," or copula, appears when both plant and animal are transcended in man.[2] In one work it is maintained that the life of plants constitutes a kind of magnetism elevated above the earth and oriented toward the sun,[3] but that in the animals the sun is typified in the brain, which fact gives rise to an opposite orientation. Certain relations between the astronomical systems are declared to be reproduced in organisms; satellites typify the structure of plants,[4] and comets are the infusoria of astronomy.[5] In the organisms the processes of reproduction are sometimes said to be akin to magnetism;[6] irritability is held to be akin to electricity;[7] and sensibility is sometimes said to be akin to chemical processes.[8] Each sense has its particular correspondences among the processes of gravitation, electricity, etc.[9] The animal instincts, since they relate to the ground of existence, are akin to gravitation.[10] In general, the organism serves as a link between two worlds, the cosmogonic and the psychological;[11] the human organism makes thinking possible.[12] The world is the permanent, while man is the temporary instance of the threefold copula of things.[13] That representation which could not be attained in plants and animals, because of their fragmentary natures, is at length attained in man, who is "absolute, potenzlose Identität," the expression of infinite substance. In this respect, man should afford the subject-matter of a new science, anthroposophy, which would be quite different from anthropology.[14] More than the plants and the animals, man exhibits well marked differentiations of upper and lower, front and back, and right and left portions of his body; he may be called the most perfect cube of nature. This "cube" of three dimensions nature has endeavored to duplicate in the brain.[15] Man represents the relation of the general, of the subject, which in him corresponds to time and the square, to the particular, the object, which corresponds to space and the cube; hence man is the immediate image of the universe.[16] Man's

---

[1] *System;* VI, 381.  [2] *Weltseele;* II, 375–376. *Cf. System;* VI, 406 ff.
[3] *System;* VI, 409.  [4] *Ibid.,* VI, 485.  [5] *Ibid.,* VI, 482.
[6] *Ibid.,* VI, 400.  [7] *Ibid.,* VI, 418.
[8] *Ibid.,* VI, 430. *Cf. Deduktion;* IV, 74, and Falckenberg, *Hist. of Mod. Philos.,* p. 453.
[9] *System;* VI, 443–449.  [10] *Ibid.,* VI, 462.  [11] *Einleitung;* III, 274.
[12] *Entwurf;* III, 169.  [13] *Weltseele;* II, 376.
[14] *System;* VI, 487–8.  [15] *Ibid.,* VI, 489.  [16] *Ibid.,* VI, 490.

body is a diminutive picture of the earth and the heavens. As in the case of the living universe, man's digestive and reproductive organs are on the inside, while his sense organs (which correspond to the sun) and his muscles (which correspond to the planets) are directed outwards. As the motions of the heavenly bodies are related to their inner identity, so articulate language is related to reason. Man is accordingly

> "the model of all living things; the harmony . . . of the universe is incorporated in him. . . . He is the center . . . and therefore in immediate inner communion and identity with all things which he is to know. All motions of the great or the little nature are concentrated in him, all forms of actuality, all qualities of earth and heavens. He is, in a word, the system of the universe, the fulness of infinite substance on a small scale—that is, the integrated being, man become God." [1]

Schelling's philosophy of nature belongs in a still larger triadic setting, where, with the "Transcendentalphilosophie" it is synthesized in "Identitätsphilosophie." In the works in which the last-named is developed, the views which have been mentioned above are overlaid with social, historical, and mystical considerations, in which Schelling abandons himself still more irresponsibly to speculation. This was, of course, the chief difficulty with his philosophy of nature, although in judging him here one should remember how many of the commonplaces of present day science, as regards both method and content, have been elaborated since his time.

*3. Theories Held by Some of Schelling's Friends.* The influence of Schelling was immediate; some of his friends produced even more remarkable speculations than his. Notable among them was Heinrich Steffens (1773–1845), who tried to present man in continuity with the whole of nature, with particular reference to facts of geology and chemistry as then understood. Steffens thought that the relations of substances in his cohesion series, together with relations of polarity, reappeared in plants and animals.[2] The central point of all organization he declared to be man; any individual organizations outside man must be regarded as scattered portions of man's organization, and must be studied in connection with man.[3] In some of his later works Steffens

---

[1] *System;* VI, 491–2.

[2] *Beiträge zur inneren Naturgeschichte der Erde* (1801); see Erdmann, *op. cit.*, vol. II, pp. 632–633.

[3] *Anthropologie* (Breslau, 1822), vol. I, preface. *Cf.* Erdmann, II, p. 634.

elaborated a philosophy of religion. As humanity is related to the All, so is Christ related to humanity. In creation three moments are to be distinguished—the cosmical, when the planets ranged themselves about the sun; the telluric, as earth found its central point in man; and the historical, when Christ appeared as the Sun of humanity.[1] Lorenz Oken (1779–1851) developed Schelling's philosophy particularly in the direction of biology. He held that the bodies of the solar system have separated themselves from the original matter by a polar linear action, or differentiation from a common center.[2] The organic world, too, arises from a chaos—*i. e.*, the infusoria,[3] and develops by similar processes.[4] The organic world is the inorganic, concentrated;[5] all organisms must resemble the universe.[6] (In other works, Oken says that in plants the planetary life, and in animals the cosmic life repeats itself.[7]) In a speculation which reminds one of Paracelsus it is said that there is not an organ in nature which is not imitated in the little nature—the earth-principle appears in the animal kingdom variously, as covering, feeling, and worms; the air, as skin, eyes, and insects; water, as lungs, touch and reptiles; metals as bones, ears, and birds; sulphur, as livers, noses, and fish; salt, as stomachs, tongues, amphibia, etc.[8] Oken thinks that animals ought to be classified according to the occurrence in them of characteristic sense-organs; but his classification varies.[9] Man unites in himself, and is a focus for everything which is divided among the other species.[10] Oken noticed in the human embryo processes later interpreted by the "recapitulation theory"—at various stages of evolution the embryo is a polyp, a plant, and an animal.[11] He had also a curious anatomical theory, according to which the head, with its various features, was said to be a repetition of the trunk, with its contents.[12] He maintained that it was as justifiable to call the senses the qualities of the universe which in man, for example, have become inward, as to say that the universe is a continua-

---

[1] Erdmann, *op. cit.*, II, 638.

[2] P. C. Mitchell, art., " Evolution," *Encyc. Brit.* (11), vol. X, p. 28.

[3] Oken, *Die Zeugung* (Bamberg and Wurzburg, 1805), p. 2.

[4] *Ibid.*, pp. 188–191.    [5] *Ibid.*, p. 186.    [6] *Ibid.*, p. 148.

[7] *Das Universum als Fortsetzung des Sinnessystems* (Jena, 1808); see Erdmann, *op. cit.*, vol. II, p. 654; Oken, *Lehrb. der Naturphilos.* (Jena, 1809–10), vol. II, §§ 817, 911, 954 ff, 975, 1780.

[8] *Die Zeugung*, pp. 175–176.

[9] *Ibid.*, p. 175. See R. Owen, art., " Oken," *Encyc. Brit.* (11), vol. XX, p. 54.

[10] *Die Zeugung*, p. 1.    [11] *Ibid.*, pp. 169, ff.

[12] See Owen, *Encyc. Brit.*, (11) XX, p. 56.

tion of the senses.[1]  The world process is not merely the antecedent condition of sensation; it is its concomitant.  What the universe does, the sensation does along with it on a small scale.[2]  Each process of the "Ur-Welt" passes over into the "Nach-Welt" as a specific sensation—for example, light becomes sight in the organism.[3]  The brain is a repetition of the stomach and lungs; thinking is its digestion, phantasy its breathing.[4]  Schelling's friend J. J. Wagner (1775–1841), in his methodical *Organon* (1851), and its later *Erläuterungen* reduced the world to 120 Ideas which form the branches of the tree of life.[5]  Instead of the triadic formula, Wagner uses a tetradic scheme of Nature, Opposition, Adjustment, Form,[6] which is found in the relations of God, Intelligence, Substance, and the All,[7] and also recurs in physiological[8] and psychological processes.[9]  In this group also belongs K. C. F. Krause (1781–1832), the originator of panentheism.  He thinks that the farther science progresses, the more there is revealed the similarity of the life of nature with that of reason, and the parallelism of their powers and work.  This parallelism is necessary and permanent, since each exhibits the same nature of God,[10] who holds the two together.[11]  Structural parallelisms are also found—according to Krause, the universe is an organic whole, rich in independent members, in which all the members are well-ordered and connected on every side.  The human body, too, is in its way a complete likeness of the universe; a religious sense has rightly called it the "little world."[12]  The earth has processes which resemble organic processes.[13]  Again, the organic world is an organism, a body, of which the plants and animals are members.[14]  Human society is also an organic whole, in which individuals are members, and humanity on earth is like a spirit in a body.[15]  Moreover, the whole of our knowledge is a system (Gliedbau); and philosophy is a system of partial systems, an organism of partial organisms, as is the human body.[16]  F. Baader (1765–1841), strictly speaking, did not belong to the school of Schelling,[17] but was a theosophist and mystic.  He had views in common with the later views of Schelling, although he substituted for the triadic formula a tetradic

---

[1] Erdmann, *op. cit.*, vol. II, p. 652.

[2] *Das Universum* . . . (Jena, 1808), p. 17.      [3] *Ibid.*, p. 21.      [4] *Ibid.*, p. 5.

[5] *Erläuterungen* (Ulm, 1854), p. 137.      [6] *Organon* (Ulm, 1851), p. 2.

[7] *Erläuterungen*, part IV, p. 2.      [8] *Ibid.*, p. 104.      [9] *Ibid.*, p. 113.

[10] *Das Urbild der Menschheit* (Dresden, 1811), pp. 23–24.      [11] *Ibid.*, p. 28.

[12] *Ibid.*, p. 10.      [13] *Ibid.*, p. 41.      [14] *Ibid.*, p. 24.      [15] *Ibid.*, p. 34.

[16] *Die Lehre vom Erkennen* (Göttingen, 1836), p. 484.

[17] Erdmann, II, p. 657.

formula, adding to the warm and cold principles those of weight and breathing. These four, he declared, are operative in both the great and the little worlds.[1] An entry in his diary shows that he was at one time (1786) favorably impressed by the theory that man is a microcosm;[2] but in other writings he modified the view, claiming that man, as a mirror of divinity rather than of the cosmos, ought to be called "Mikrotheus," or "little god."[3] It is said that H. C. Oersted (1777–1851) was helped by his speculations to the discovery[4] of the deflection of the magnetic needle by the electric current; but the other speculations of the school of Schelling had little in common with achievements of this kind. The whole movement was chiefly noteworthy by reason of its aim and its enthusiasm.[5]

4. *The Attitude of Hegel toward Microcosmic Theories.* Schelling's philosophy of nature is, in general, so much like Hegel's that one might expect to find Hegel also an adherent of the microcosmic views, but the traces of them are very few. Hegel was apparently not much interested in cosmology.[6] He insisted strongly upon the concrete actuality of experience; he thought that in the study of an organism the essential thing to look for was not its place in a system, nor its character as an

---

[1] *Uber das Pythag. Quadrat in der Natur* (1798), in Baader's *Sämmtliche Werke* (Leipzig, 1852, etc.), vol. III, p. 267.

[2] *Werke*, vol. XI, p. 78.

[3] For refs. see Index, *Werke*, vol. XVI, p. 324. Baader often quotes the French mystic, L. C. de Saint Martin (1743–1803).

[4] Ueberweg-Oesterreich *Grundr. der Gesch. der Phil.*, vol. IV (Berlin, 1916), p. 699.

[5] In this connection mention may be made of a book by E. Bauer, *Symbolik des Kosmos* . . . (Weimar, 1854). Bauer held, with K. G. Carus, that spiritual truths may be presented in visible symbols without becoming involved in materialism (p. iv). The cosmos is a symbol of God (p. 7). The processes of attraction, polarization, undulation, and neutralization, as well as morphology, may be traced in both cosmic and individual lives (pp. 29–30). Minerals symbolize memory (p. 31); plants and animals symbolize man's senses (p. 37). Contemporary with the men of this period was C. Fourier (1772–1837), with his curious Pythagoreanism. He held that the harmony of human passions was reflected throughout the universe in social, animal, organic, and material movements (*Theorie des 4 mouvements* . . . in his *Oeuvres* (Paris, 1861), vol. I, pp. 29–31). Human history is outlined according to the ascending and descending "vibrations" it has passed through and must pass through (pp. 34, ff.). He based his social system upon a cosmic conception; on each planet he pictured a race of human or quasi-human beings, each having as its function the making valuable of the life of the planet and of the universe (C. Limousin, in *Annales de l'Institute de sociologie*, vol. IV—Paris, 1898—p. 322).

[6] J. E. McTaggart, *Studies in Hegelian Cosmology* (Cambridge, 1901), p. 2.

isolated image of some general reality, but the process going on in it and
the function exercised by it.[1]  In several passages he deprecates the
methods followed in the development of microcosmic theories—Paracelsus and Boehme are not to be understood "nach der Existenz," and
Schelling and Steffens have worked out suggestive but superficial co-
ordinations.[2]  Schelling's recognition of opposites in polarity is only an
empty scheme in which real development never comes by its rights.[3]  At
the same time, the triadic formula is applied in the *Encyklopädie* much
more rigidly than by Schelling, and might easily be taken as the basis of
many a microcosmic construction.  Moreover, Hegel alludes to the
earth as a dead-lying organism,[4] speaks of the individual as a world,[5]
calls the Idea an organic system, and compares philosophy itself to an
organism.[6]  But it was left for some of his interpreters to link his thought
up with the microcosmic theories more definitely than he himself did.[7]

*5. Microcosmic Theories Used by Other German Philosophers of the
Period.*  Other German thinkers in this period were more definite in their
expressions concerning microcosmic theories.  Schleiermacher developed
his ethical and religious views with the aid of such theories.  For him,
every individual thing is the work of the whole universe,[8] and contains,
by virtue of its individuality, something not found anywhere else.[9]  The
world-spirit is revealed in the smallest things as well as in the greatest,[10]
but preëminently in man's self-consciousness, which is the immediate
working of the universe.[11]  By a deepening of religious feeling one can
find within one's self everything that is working upon one from without;[12]
in the inner life, the universe portrays itself.[13]  The organization of the
human spirit is the workshop of the universe;[14] again, we are the tools of
the universe.[15]  Every individual human being is a portrait and compendium of humanity.[16]  In order to have the life of the world-spirit, in

[1] *Phänomenologie des Geistes*, in Hegel's *Werke* (Berlin, 1832, etc.), vol. II, p. 202.

[2] *Ibid.*, vol. VII (1), pp. 156–7.

[3] Höffding, *Hist. of Mod. Philos.*, II, p. 177.

[4] *Encyk.*, in *Werke*, vol. VII (1), p. 310.

[5] *Phänom.*, in *Werke*, vol. II, p. 319.

[6] *Gesch. der Philos.*, in *Werke*, vol. XIII, pp. 40–41.

[7] See Falckenberg, *Hist. of Mod. Philos.*, p. 494; Weber, *Hist. of Philos.*, pp. 510–511;
J. G. Hibben, *Hegel's Logic* (New York, 1902), p. 17.

[8] *Reden über die Religion*, . . ., in Schleiermacher's *Sämmtliche Werke* (Berlin, 1843),
Abt. I, vol. I, p. 290.

[9] *Ibid.*, I, 297.      [10] *Ibid.*, I, 226.      [11] *Ibid.*, I, 193.      [12] *Ibid.*, I, 235.

[13] *Ibid.*, I, 228.      [14] *Ibid.*, I, 287.      [15] *Ibid.*, I, 290.      [16] *Ibid.*, I, 237.

order to have religion, man must first love his fellow men. That man is most lovable in whom the world mirrors itself most clearly and most purely.[1] The microcosmic conception is here psychological rather than anatomical or physiological; it has little structural basis, and Schleiermacher lays more stress upon the development of individual qualities than upon microcosmic relations.[2] Interesting in the light of subsequent developments are Herbart's suggestive comparisons between ideas in the mind and individuals in society. Each exhibits conflicting groups, in which the many are opposed by the few, and in which various factors and elements tend to reappear at intervals. Either the ranks and orders of society, or the legislative, executive and judicial powers of the state afford suggestive analogies to the mental faculties. "If observations of this kind were completely elaborated, they would furnish a science of politics similar to empirical psychology."[3]

Schopenhauer substitutes will for the Hegelian reason, and holds that in our own experience of willing we know the impulse which produces the world and its living forms.[4] The various grades of objectification of this will extend all the way from the physical processes of pressure and resistance[5] up to man.[6]

> "If several of the phenomena of will in the lower grades of its objectification . . . come into conflict because each of them, under the guidance of causality, seeks to possess a given portion of matter, there arises from the conflict the phenomenon of a higher Idea which prevails over all the less developed phenomena previously there, yet in such a way that it allows the essence of these to continue to exist in a subordinate manner, in that it takes up into itself from them something which is analogous to them."[7]

By such progressive integration the objectification becomes more and more distinct. The forces of gravitation are subdued by those of magnetism; other grades of the conflict and objectification are seen in processes of crystallization, the relation of suns and planets, physiological processes, and the struggles between species.[8] Man alone, apart from the rest of

---

[1] *Ibid.*, I, 228–229.

[2] Falckenberg, *Hist. of Mod. Philos.*, p. 485.

[3] Herbart, *Lehrbuch der Psychologie*, sec. 240 (Eng. transl. by M. K. Smith, New York, 1896, pp. 190–191).

[4] *Über die Wille in der Natur* (Leipzig, 1867), p. 2.

[5] *The World as Will and Idea* (Eng. transl. R. Haldane, J. Kemp, London, 1888), vol. I, p. 195.

[6] *Ibid.*, vol. I, p. 403.     [7] *Ibid.*, vol. I, p. 189.     [8] *Ibid.*, vol. I, pp. 189–192.

nature, cannot express the whole being of the will,[1] but man can recognize the will, his own nature, even in the inorganic.[2]  Man has such a
degree of knowledge that his idea affords a repetition of the essence of the
world; and in man the world-will comes to fullest knowledge of itself.[3]
With his will and his ideas, each localized in the body,[4] every one is
himself on a double aspect, the whole world, the microcosm, and what he
recognizes as his own being exhausts the being of the whole world, the
macrocosm.[5]   Another thinker who takes psychology as his point of
departure is F. Beneke.  For him, four processes characteristic of the
psychical—namely (1), the construction of sensory impressions and
perceptions, (2) the addition of new elementary faculties, (3) equilibration or reciprocal transfer of elements in perceptions or representations,
and (4) combinations of mental products according to the measure of
their similarity [6]—may all be traced downward into the material world.[7]

## 6. The Panpsychism of Fechner

*1. General Statement Regarding Fechner's Theories*.  The thinkers who
were united in their opposition to subjectivism became divided among
themselves on the questions of materialism as against spiritualism.
Fechner attempted the panpsychist's answer, and in developing it
elaborated microcosmic theories in more detail, and in a more striking
manner, than any other writer, ancient or modern.  His views may be
summed up by saying that men, astronomical bodies, and the universe as
a whole are to be considered both corporeally and spiritually,[8] and that,
when they are considered in this way, men in their relations to the earth
are as the earth and the other astronomical bodies are in their relations
to the universe as a whole.  The spirit of the universe as a whole is known

---

[1] *The World as Will and Idea*, vol. I, p. 200.        [2] *Ibid*., vol. I, p. 153.

[3] *Ibid*., vol. I, pp. 370–371.        [4] *Ibid*., vol. I, p. 262.

[5] *Ibid*., vol. I, p. 212; the terms are also found in vol. I, pp. 427–428, and vol. III,
p. 404.  *Cf*. also vol. I, p. 237. In connection with Schopenhauer's microcosmic theories
mention should be made of his magnificent metaphor comparing the universe to a
symphony orchestra (*Ibid*., vol. II, p. 209; vol. III, pp. 330, ff.).

[6] Beneke, *Lehrbuch der Psychologie* (Berlin, 1861), pp. 16, 18, 19, 26.

[7] Falckenberg, *Hist. of Mod. Philos*., p. 512.

[8] *Zend-Avesta* (Leipzig, 1851–1854), vol. I, p. 469.  Unless otherwise specified, all
citations from Fechner refer to volume and page of this work. References may be
found by following this paging, which is given in the third edition (ed. by K. Lasswitz,
Hamburg and Leipzig, 1906).

to us as God.   Once, in a passage later somewhat qualified, he uses the terms "macrocosm" and "microcosm"—saying that we have rocks in our bones, streams running through our arteries, light penetrating our eyes, and perhaps some fine force coursing in our nerves; [1] but his importance for the history of microcosmic theories is much greater than this single passage indicates.

2. *Fechner's Use of the Method of Analogy.*   Fechner is careful to say that he brings no proofs for his views; the whole thing must remain a matter of faith, but he thinks that no one will find a more natural, clearer, simpler point of view. [2]   Even though one might not be able to appeal with confidence to any single argument which he puts forward, he holds that there is a certain strength in their total effect. [3]   The view is an extension rather than a contradiction of those already established. [4]   He is aware of some of the limitations of the method of analogy; everything is, in some respects, like everything else, but in other respects it is different; one must be careful to specify the respects in which he would point out resemblances. [5]   While every reasonable analogy helps, [6] and while sometimes there are even analogies between series of unlike things, [7] still analogy is never as useful as teleology, [8] and serves only as the first approach to more direct knowledge. [9]   Since final dependence is not placed upon the method of analogy, one should not be a slave of the method, but should vary one's analogies in order to develop suggestive points of view. [10]   Like everything new, the method is precarious; but one has no safety apart from it. [11]

3. *Theories of Resemblances between the Earth and the Human Organism.* With some cautions and reservations such as the foregoing, Fechner proceeds to develop nearly fifty numbered points concerning resemblances between the earth and the human organism.   They resemble one another, in that each arises from a flux; [12] each continues in an environment (in the case of the earth, the æther); [13] each partakes of a force which is general, applying it within the limits of individuality [14] (in the case of the earth, the force is that of gravity); each develops from a greater body by a process of differentiation; [15] each depends for existence upon a

---

[1] *Zend-Avesta*, I, pp. 102–103.

[2] I, 224–225.    [3] *Ibid.*, and I, 288; III, p. v.    [4] I, 470.    [5] I, 64.

[6] III, pp. iv, 45.    [7] III, 8.

[8] *Die Tagesansicht gegenüber der Nachtansicht* (Leipzig, 1904), p. 34.

[9] *Zend-Avesta*, III, iii.    [10] I, 70–71, 283.    [11] III, p. v.    [12] I, 132.

[13] *Tagesansicht*, p. 31.    [14] *Zend-Avesta*, I, 136–137.    [15] I, 51.

father, and the universe; [1] each is linked to other individuals by species relationships; [2] each incorporates its materials into a continuing and definitely coördinated individual whole; [3] each has rhythmic [4] and circulatory [5] processes; each passes through definite periods of development; [6] each differs in its various parts according to the form of aggregation of its component parts; [7] each receives influences from other individuals of its class, and by the help of these perfects within itself certain structures which, though subordinate to it, constitute its highest part; [8] and each differentiates within itself a special region which is the locus of outward action and upward striving (in the earth, this is the organic kingdom—in man, it is the head, with the brain and sense organs).[9] Besides such analogies, there are also some interesting compound analogies between the earth and the human organism; it may be said that within certain limits, terrestrial creatures are related to the earth as our sense organs are to us.[10]   Just as the body must help to produce an image, so the earth must help to produce man.[11]   Just as the earth does not bring forth any new species of living organisms, so man does not produce any new roots for words.[12]   Just as our sensations of change affect the whole body, so our activities affect the whole earth.[13]   There is some question concerning freedom, but both the earth and man can bring forth new processes as well as old.[14]   As the individual will is greater than the sum of separate motives, so the will of the earth-spirit is greater than the sum of separate individuals within it.[15]   As ideas can go contrary to the will of the person who has them, so we may go contrary to the higher spiritual entities which contain us.[16]   Just as a man receives communications (sound-waves) from another by means of his sense organs, so the earth may be said to receive communications (light-waves) from other astronomical bodies by means of the plants, animals, and men which it contains; we may suppose here that in the case of the earth, as in that of the man, the waves taken separately convey little meaning, and also that the light-waves mean something different to the planet than they do to us.[17]   Men are apparently much more closely related to one another than are the astronomical bodies; but perhaps the actions of the latter upon one another are after all more immediate.[18]

---

[1] I, 317.          [2] I, 157; *cf.* I, 49, 95, and *Tagesansicht*, p. 32.
[3] I, 49–51.          [4] I, 50, 125.          [5] I, 121.          [6] I, 126.
[7] I, 102; *cf.* I, 136, 429, and *Tagesansicht*, p. 37.          [8] I, 167.          [9] I, 52.          [10] I, 286.
[11] III, 5.          [12] I, 231.          [13] I, 130–131.          [14] I, 168–180.          [15] I, 302.
[16] I, 36–38.          [17] I, 175–176.          [18] I, 166–167.

*4. Explanations for Obvious Differences between Earth and Human Organism.* Fechner finds that no analogy between the earth and man can be entirely applicable; [1] but nevertheless, some of the differences between them can be explained. Among these are, first, the differences of degree. Of course the earth is on a much grander and more complex scale than man; [2] but these differences, far from showing that the earth is not an organism, show that it is an organism of a higher order. [3] Moreover, the earth would be at a disadvantage if its lungs, stomach, and brain were in the interior, because the way leading to them would then be too long; we must look for these organs, if at all, near the surface. [4] The absence of a nervous system in the earth merely shows that the earth has not a human soul. [5] Sometimes the differences are accounted for in terms of the compound analogies; thus it is said that our bones are like rocks, but are not real rocks, but that, since the human body is the most highly developed organ of the earth, we must expect to find more complications in us than outside us. [6] Again, the earth's (geological) movements are great, compared to our movements; but even so, the movements of our muscles are great, compared to the bodily changes which sustain our ideas. [7] Again, it is said that the earth is quieter than man, but that, also, man's body is quieter than his nerves, or the circulation of his blood. [8] Sometimes the differences between earth and man are traced to the part-whole relation between them; [9] man cannot expect to repeat the whole earth on a small scale, but only to present one finer portion of the whole. [10] Sometimes, finally, the differences between the earth and man are explained in terms which imply the continuity of their processes; it is said that the earth has lungs and brains, for example, in the very fact that men who inhabit the earth have them. [11] To be sure, the brains of individual men do not combine into one earth-brain; but in a human organism the separate nerves do not combine into one single nerve, either. [12] By virtue of such a relation of continuity as this, the earth may be said to run, eat, and cry. [13] The earth has a slight degree of sensation when the plants have sensations; a somewhat greater degree when the animals have sensations; but more is mirrored in a living way in the experiences of mankind. [14] At the same time Fechner refuses to say that the earth's reason is the sum of human reasons. [15]

[1] I, 283.　　[2] I, 53; *cf.* I, 16, 57–58, 91, 284.　　[3] I, 60–62.　　[4] I, 82, 167.
[5] I, 211.　　[6] I, 103.　　[7] I, 74; *cf.* I, 26, and *Tagesansicht*, p. 37.　　[8] I, 105.
[9] I, 53; *cf. Tagesansicht*, p. 30.　　[10] I, 79; *cf.* I, 63.　　[11] I, 63.　　[12] I, 215.
[13] I, 215; *cf.* II, 207.　　[14] I, 287; *cf.* I, 283.　　[15] I, 190.

*5. Other Differences between Earth and Organism, Left Unexplained.*
Fechner recognized the weaknesses of some of his analogies without
attempting to account for them. For example, he says that although the
sea with its tides is like a beating heart, and the rivers and the brooks are
like arteries and capillaries, and the atmosphere into which the water is
periodically evaporated is like the lungs, and although in the case of the
earth the geological processes, and in the case of man the physiological
processes are connected with the foregoing, still, the comparison breaks
down. The heart drives blood into all the arteries, but the tides do not
appear in all rivers. Moreover, the tides go around the earth in a special
way, different from that of the blood in the body. The tides are due to
external influence acting upon the earth, but the pulse is not due to
external influence. And the water is not oxydized in the atmosphere as
the venous blood is in the lungs.[1] Again, some of the differences of degree are accentuated. The principal masses of nerves and muscles in the
body tend to form aggregates, just as animals do in the earth. The
viscera sometimes show branching structures, as the plants do, and the
skeleton bears some resemblances to earth's rocks. But these resemblances are offset by differences; by means of an animal's nerves and
muscles, the skeleton can be moved, while we of course do not move the
earth—and on the other hand, plants work over relatively little of the
matter surrounding them, compared to the amount worked over by our
digestive systems.[2] The earth does not waste away, as does the human
body.[3] For us, winter and summer are differences of time, but for the
earth they are differences of place;[4] the earth has the entire content of
our consciousness before it, but we have not the entire content of its
consciousness before us.[5] All the cyclic processes of the earth, having as
their limit, its rotation, are confined to the earth; but all man's cyclic
processes are not confined to the individual's body.[6] Again, man is not
self-sufficient, as is the earth; still, it must be admitted that the earth has
some outer relations.[7]

*6. Analogies between Earth and Organism Extended to the Universe.*
Although he recognizes such differences as those noted above, Fechner
extends his analogies between the earth and the organism to the universe
also. The extension is not made without some reservations; the fact, for
instance, that the solar system is superior to the earth system involves

[1] I, 64–66; the comparisons vary—see I, 71, 126, 283.
[2] I, 66.     [3] I, 73; cf. I, 176–177.     [4] I, 55.   [5] I, 295; cf. I, 115.
[6] I, 122.        [7] I, 54–56, 91–95.

relations different from those found in the fact that the earth is superior to our bodies.[1]  Whereas the earth must be admitted to have some external relations, the universe is utterly independent.[2]  The stars in the universe are not very closely related to one another; men in the earth are more closely related to one another; and the organs of the body of an individual man are much more closely related to one another.[3]  The analogy which holds between man and the earth breaks down at some points when applied to God.[4]  But, for all these reservations, one may say that the earth and each star are cells in the body of the universe;[5] or, again, that as a man brings forth images and ideas within the unity of his consciousness, so the earth brings forth the man and other living beings within its unity, and so God brings forth the earth and the stars in his unity.[6]  The parallelism is strictly dualistic: human spirits belong to a higher earth-spirit which binds everything earthly in one, and this spirit belongs in turn to God, who binds the whole universe in one; on the other hand, our bodies are parts of the earth-body, and the earth-body is part of the divine body of nature.  The earth is thus a body and spirit intermediate between God and man.[7]  Man is an offshoot and representation (Bild) of the whole God-animated universe, although immediately he is an offspring of the earth.[8]

7. *Use of these Analogies as Basis for Christian Doctrines.*  Upon a basis of such analogies Fechner worked out in considerable detail theories covering some of the important Christian doctrines.  His argument concerning the work of Christ may be stated as follows. an individual man has many ideas of various degrees of importance, but in his experience there may come one idea which gives a supreme direction to his entire life and thought, and with which all his subsequent ideas and acts are linked up.  Even when long sought for, the appearance of the preeminent idea is often sudden.  It takes time for the preeminent idea to prevail over the others, but when it does prevail it brings peace and unity and correlated development.  The preeminent idea is, in fact, a mediator between the individual in whose experience it occurs, and something super-individual, superior, controlling; the idea could not exercise its controlling functions without such reference.  But the idea need not always be in conscious relation with the other ideas of the individual; the fact that it appeared once in ordinary consciousness suffices to establish its contact with other succeeding states, and its controlling function.

[1] II, 244.   [2] I, 56, 105.   [3] I, 165.   [4] I, 302, 309.   [5] I, 100.
[6] I, 44-45, 224, II, 244.   [7] II, 1, 2.   [8] III, 5.

may continue long after it has disappeared, and after the outward circumstances which called it forth have been altered. Perhaps not every man has such an idea; but the nature of each individual is fragmentary, and needs to be supplemented by the ideas of other men.[1] Now, since ideas in the experience of an individual may be set in parallel with individuals in the history of the earth, we may say that a preëminent man, Christ, has appeared and lived among men, and given to subsequent history a direction, and linked his followers with himself, bringing peace and unity.[2] He is a mediator between us and God,[3] but need not be always upon the earth, as he was at first.[4] Christ as he was in his earthly incarnation does not appear in other stars, but the Word must probably be made flesh in other stars as well as in the earth.[5] Fechner devoted much attention to a theory of life after death, which was also worked out in accordance with his analogies.[6] The life of a man is related to the earth as, for example, a visual sensation is related to the body; the earth, together with its environment (the universe, or God), must help to produce man, just as the body, with its environment, must help to produce a sensation.[7] The death of a man is related to the earth as, for example, the discontinuance of a visual sensation is related to the body; and man's life after death is related to the earth as a memory of a visual sensation is related to the body.[8] Just as the individual brain brings forth what was essential in the sensation after the eyes are closed, so the earth brings forth what was essential in the individual after death.[9] As memories persist in spite of the fact that new sensations are using the same nerve paths, so individuals persist after death, in spite of the fact that later individuals may have incorporated into their bodies the same materials.[10] As all memories are to some degree associated in the experience of an individual, so all individuals will be more or less associated in the life after death; but there will be in the latter, as in the former case, certain laws of association.[11] As our memories do not awaken all at once, but await appropriate conditions, so we may suppose that the life of individuals after death sometimes awaits appropriate conditions.[12] Just as it is by the aid of memory that the language of men is understood, so it may be by our aid that the communications of the heavenly spheres will become intelligible.[13] Fechner has a unique theory concerning the

---

[1] II, 54–57.  [2] II, 58.  [3] II, 53.  [4] II, 62–64.
[5] II, 61–62.  [6] See *Tagesansicht*, pp. 99–100.  [7] III, 4–5.  [8] III, 7–8.
[9] III, 9.  [10] *Tagesansicht*, pp. 99–100.  [11] III, 53–54, 193.
[12] *Tagesansicht*, p. 94; *cf.* III, 329.  [13] III, 51.

conditions of life after death. As the corporeal elements of memory, whatever they are, grow out of those of perception, so the corporeal elements of a future life grow out of those of present life.[1] In the case of the earth we find that, in spite of our ordinary view, the matter upon which a man works during his lifetime forms a spatial and temporal continuum.[2] There is thus a material and spatial continuity between Christ and us; we know it in the Church (the body of Christ), the Scriptures, and the sacraments.[3] Man during his lifetime makes a place for himself in the earth,[4] leaves his impression upon the matter upon which he has worked; this is his "body" in the life after death.[5] In the next life we shall have the form of the present body, without being burdened by its matter.[6] Nor does the future "body" depend merely upon the outer impression made by each individual in the material of the earth; for we all work not merely upon the earth, but also upon one another here, and we all help to reconstitute one another in the new life.[7] There is, however, something more than mere analogies involved; for our "memory-life" here can be regarded as the germ (Keim) of our "memory-life" in the hereafter.[8]

8. *The Influence of Fechner.* Fechner felt that his work, the "day-view" as opposed to the "night-view" of the empirical and materialistic sciences, combined satisfactorily the results of studies of nature from different points of view; that it had a certain strength because, after all, it restated a view that was primitive; and that it formed a consistent system, rather than a patchwork;[9] and that in it science and theology were of mutual assistance.[10] But for most of the thinkers who have succeeded him, his analogies have been too loose and his panpsychism, in spite of his elaborate arguments for it, has been too fantastic. Moreover, the sciences since his time have been occupied almost exclusively with the study of the accumulating data of evolution, until there has been little time or interest in correlations in accordance with any other principle. The result has been that, except for Paulsen, whose work will be noted below, Fechner has had no notable following. But William James found in him a man who had vision, who gave the impression of one who did not live at second hand, who made some other systems of philosophy appear thin by comparison, and who was "a philosopher in the great sense."[11]

---

[1] III, 390.  [2] III, 120.  [3] III, 120–124, 363–370.  [4] III, 52.
[5] III, 124–128, 131.  [6] III, 145.  [7] III, 160–165.  [8] III, 46.  [9] I, p. xiv.
[10] II, 67.  [11] *A Pluralistic Universe* (New York, 1909), pp. 149, 154, 165, 176.

## 7. THE "MICROCOSMUS" OF LOTZE

*1. General Position of Lotze.* Another answer to the problems of materialism and mechanism and empiricism was attempted by Lotze, the title of whose masterpiece affords the instance of the use of the term "microcosm" which is best known at the present day. From the point of view of the history of the microcosmic theories, however, the term is used in a restricted sense, and should be studied in the Lotzian setting. This may be indicated by saying that Lotze proposes a system of centers of force, which, except for the fact that they interact, are like the monads of Leibnitz, and each of which is a mirror of the universe.[1] "To be" means to stand in relations;[2] to exchange actions;[3] to be causes;[4] to be modes of one substance;[5] and, if we wish to understand nature, we must say, to be at least in some degree akin to the nature of mind.[6] Mechanism, although universal in extent, is negligible in importance;[7] it is the condition of the mind's thought of itself,[8] but is transcended in the unity of the soul, which is evident in the fact that we are able to appear to ourselves.[9] "Living beings alone truly are; the other forms of existence derive their explanation solely from mental life, not the latter from them."[10] Only the full reality of an infinite living being has power to knit together the multiplicity of things and to enable reciprocal actions to take place.[11] The universal is, however, inferior as compared with the particular, and any state of things is insignificant as compared with the good arising from its enjoyment.[12]

*2. Lotze's Strictures on Older Microcosmic Theories.* Lotze's estimate of mechanism leaves him with scant sympathy for views which maintain that there is an immediate and mysterious sympathy between man and nature, particularly man and the earth, or that powers and tendencies of development inherent in the earth are repeated in more significant forms in the bodies of men, or that the internal fluctuations of telluric life find echoes in changes of human organization, or that what the earth vainly struggles to express receives a spiritualized manifestation in the constitution of conscious beings. He thinks that these views owe their convincing power to men's strange inclination to regard the unintelligible and undemonstrable as having preëminent truth and profundity.[13] It is perverse

---

[1] *Microcosmus* (first published 1856–64). Eng. transl. by E. Hamilton and E. C. Jones, Edinburgh, 1887, vol. I, pp. 359–360.

[2] *Ibid.*, II, 578 ff.    [3] II, 617, ff.    [4] II, 598.    [5] II, 598.
[6] II, 647–648 and ff.    [7] I, p. xvi.    [8] II, 658.    [9] I, 157.
[10] I, 362.    [11] I, 380.    [12] II, 728.    [13] II, 7.

to compare the earth's day and night to the waking and sleep of an organism.[1] The *Microcosmus* renews a warfare, which Lotze had "begun long ago," against the inclination to see in every individual department of reality merely an imitative echo or a prophetic indication of some other department, and in the whole great circle of phenomena only a continuous shading forth of the higher by the lower, or the lower by the higher.[2] He felt that the attempt to model the duties of creatures which have minds upon the phenomena of the external world was a barren blunder of sentimental symbolism, and could further nothing but the establishment of ordinary conditions.[3] Enclosed within the great machine of nature stands the smaller machine of the human mind, more cunningly framed than any other,[4] yet physical events and conscious states are absolutely incompatible.[5] Man is a living product, unique in kind, receiving innumerable impressions from nature, that he may be roused by them to reactions and developments, the cause of which lies in himself.[6]

*3. Lotze's Use of the Term "Microcosm."* Lotze's most distinctive view of man as the microcosm has theological and ethical rather than physical or physiological implications.

"As in the great fabric of the universe the Creative Spirit imposed on itself unchangeable laws by which it moves the world of phenomena, diffusing the fulness of the Highest Good throughout innumerable forms and events, and distilling it again from them into the bliss of consciousness and enjoyment; so must man, acknowledging the same laws, develop given existence into a knowledge of its value, and the value of his ideals into a series of external forms proceeding from himself. . . . In the energy of a freedom that does not aimlessly stray and desire the fruit without the slow growth of the plant, but consciously restraining himself within the firm bounds of necessity which he holds sacred, and following the tracks prescribed to him, . . . man will be that which, according to an ancient idea, he is above all creatures—the complete reflection of the great real world, the little world, the *Microcosm*." [7]

In volume II the term "microcosmic order" is introduced to describe "the impulses, ever fresh and ever the same, out of which have sprung the many-hued blossoms of history, the eternal cycle in which human

[1] II, 8.    [2] II, 20–21.    [3] II, 22.    [4] I, 25.
[5] I, 148, 161–163, 195.    [6] II, 21.
[7] I, 401.

fates revolve." [1]  It is evidently in the light of these passages that one is
to read the statement in the introduction to the effect that

> "As the growing farsightedness of astronomy dissipated the idea that
> the great theatre of human life was in direct connection with divinity,
> so the further advance of mechanical science begins to threaten with
> similar disintegration the smaller world, the *Microcosm of man*." [2]

The title of the book was apparently chosen with such views in mind;
and it is clear that these uses of the term microcosm are, especially when
compared with Fechner's, loose. [3]  In the sense in which the two words
are often used, one could say that Fechner's microcosmic theories are
predominantly structural, while Lotze's are functional.

### 8. MICROCOSMIC THEORIES AND THE THEORY OF EVOLUTION

*1. Spencer's "First Principles."*  The next great figure in philosophy
marks the emergence of an absorbing new interest, which does much to
turn attention from the problems raised by Fechner and Lotze.  Herbert
Spencer's elaborate exposition of the processes and law of evolution
carried illustrations from, and applications to various classes of "phenomena"—astronomical, geological, biological, psychological, and sociological. [4]  All these exhibit attractions and repulsions, [5] rhythm, [6] segregation
of like elements, [7] which involves aggregation and secondary distributions,
or differentiations, [8] equilibration, [9] with internal motions of redistribu-
tion and composition, [10] and dissolution. [11]  The whole process is, however,
one of cosmic oscillation, and alternation between epochs of evolution
and dissolution. [12]  Thus Spencer was led to the conclusion that

> "the entire process of things, as displayed in the aggregate of the
> visible universe, is analogous to the entire process of things as dis-
> played in the smallest aggregates." [13]

---

[1] II, 5.     [2] I, p. xv.

[3] In spite of Lotze's dominant tendencies, there are passages which remind one of
Fechnerian and other analogies.  Both the living forms and mental life show associa-
tions (I, 367).  Social groups are rightly called organic formations (I, 438).  The
Infinite Being is stimulated from within by the production of living forms and reacts
by endowing them with souls; but this stimulation does not proceed by paths and
centers (I, 390–391).  In his "*Seéle und Seelenleben*" (1846; in *Kleine Schriften*, ed.
by D. Peiper, Leipzig, 1886, vol. II, p. 199), Lotze refers to the body as a microcosm.

[4] *First Principles* (New York, 1896), part II, chaps. XIV–XVII.

[5] *Ibid.*, chap. IX.

[6] *Ibid.*, chap. X.     [7] Chap. XXI.     [8] Chap. XIV, sec. 115.     [9] Chap. XXII.
[10] Chap. XVII.     [11] Chap. XXIII.     [12] Chap. XXIII, sec. 183.     [13] *Ibid.*

Such a conclusion as this might have led other writers directly to micro-cosmic theories, but for a number of reasons Spencer did not develop his thought in this direction. His emphasis upon a theory of knowledge made him regard the data of the sciences as "phenomena," the real nature of which was unknowable.[1] His antipathy for Hegelianism made him antagonize a tendency to "decipher the universe as the autobiography of an Infinite Spirit, repeating itself in miniature within our Finite Spirit." [2] He was concerned in demonstrating the continuity and unity of the evolutionary process as a whole, rather than in studying the resemblances between its various component processes;

"While we think of Evolution as divided into astronomic, geologic, biologic, psychologic, sociologic, etc., it may seem to a certain extent a coincidence that the same law of metamorphosis holds throughout all its divisions. But when we recognize these divisions as mere conventional groupings, made to facilitate the arrangement and acquisition of knowledge . . . we see at once that there are not several kinds of Evolution having certain traits in common, but one Evolution going on everywhere after the same manner." [3]

Although Spencer saw that astronomical bodies, like organisms, exhibit structural differentiations accompanying their integrations, he thought the processes were so slow and simple that they might be disregarded.[4] Thus materials which might have been used in the construction of a microcosmic theory more imposing than that of Fechner were reduced to the status of illustrations of the one all-absorbing process of evolution.

2. *Spencer's "Principles of Sociology."* Analogies are more prominent in Spencer's theory of society. A society is to be regarded as an entity because its parts exhibit persistent relations,[5] and these relations are analogous to those of an organism.[6] Societies, like living bodies, originate from masses which are extremely minute in comparison with the masses which some of them eventually reach.[7] In each case there is increase by simple multiplication of units, by union of groups, and by union of groups of groups.[8] Growth is accompanied in each case by increasing unlikeness of parts,[9] which are in relations of mutual dependence.[10] A society, like a living being, may survive successive lives and deaths of its component

[1] Chap. XXIV, sec. 194.     [2] Pt. I, chap. V, sec. 31.     [3] Chap. XXIV, sec. 188.
[4] *Principles of Sociology* (3 vols., New York, 1909–1912), sec. 215.
[5] *Ibid.*, sec. 212.
[6] *Ibid.*, sec. 213.     [7] Sec. 224.     [8] Sec. 226.     [9] Sec. 223; *cf.* sec. 230.
[10] Sec. 223; *cf.* sec. 235.

units.[1] In the living organism, and in society, there are in general three types of organs, the sustaining, the distributing, and the regulating; in a society these are, respectively, the industrial, the commercial, and the directive and defensive systems.[2] Organs in organisms and organs in societies have internal arrangements framed on the same principle; there are in each case appliances for conveying nutriment, for bringing materials, for carrying away the product, etc.[3] The stages of progressive specialization are parallel;[4] but in each case, organs may appear in higher forms without going through all the earlier stages.[5] With all his analogies, Spencer points out two or three important differences between biological organisms and societies. The subordinate units of the society are discrete, although this difference is greatly modified by language.[6] Again, societies are asymmetrical.[7] In a society, also, conciousness is diffused through all the constituent members, and there is no specialized seat of feeling and thought.[8] These differences help to give point to Spencer's insistence that there exist "no analogies between the body politic and a living body, save those necessitated by that mutual dependence of parts which they display in common."[9] He declares that although he has made comparisons of social structures and functions to structures and functions in the human body, these comparisons have been made only because the latter structures and functions furnish familiar illustrations of structures and functions in general.

"All kinds of creatures are alike in so far as each exhibits coöperation among its components for the benefit of the whole; . . . this . . . is common also to societies. Further, among individual organisms, the degree of coöperation measures the degree of evolution; . . . this general truth, too, holds among social organisms. Once more, to effect increasing coöperation, creatures of every order show us increasingly-complex appliances for transfer and mutual influence; and to this general characteristic, societies of every order furnish a corresponding characteristic. These, then, are the analogies alleged:

[1] Sec. 223.        [2] Sec. 238, ff.        [3] Sec. 231.
[4] Sec. 232, ff., *cf.* sec. 252.        [5] Sec. 233.
[6] Secs. 220–221. In an early article (*Westminster Review*, vol. LXXIII, 1860), Spencer removes an apparent objection concerning differences in the mobility of constituent parts of an organism and the state by saying that in the latter the citizens are fixed in their public capacities (p. 51). His general conclusion is that points of difference between the two serve to bring into clearer light the points of analogy (p. 56; *cf. Princ. of Sociol.*, sec. 269, n.).
[7] Sec. 269.        [8] Sec. 222.        [9] Sec. 269.

community in the fundamental principles of organization is the only community asserted." [1]

He means the organismic theory to serve only as a scaffold for his sociology; [2] and he appeals to both resemblance [3] and difference [4] between society and an organism, as support for his individualism.

*3. The Term "Microcosm" Used by Darwin and Huxley.* Of the other great leaders of the evolutionists, Darwin used the term microcosm to describe the constitution of multicellular organisms, made up of great numbers of smaller units.[5] Huxley compared the organism to an army, and said that in the fact that disease might be traced either to individual cells or to the arrangements for their coördination "the microcosm repeats the macrocosm," since the inefficiency of an army might be traced to similar causes.[6] In his *Evolution and Ethics*, even when he declares that the cosmic process, with its ruthlessness and resulting survivals of the fittest, is not to be a pattern for human social actions, and that men are not to imitate the cosmic process but to combat it, he still uses the microcosmic terminology.[7]

## 9. SUMMARY: MICROCOSMIC THEORIES FROM DESCARTES TO SPENCER

The course of development covered by this chapter has been indicated in the opening section, above. The ancient microcosmic theories which had been revived in various settings during the early modern period, were first eclipsed by subjectivism, then, with the trend toward objectivism, revived in the theories of Herder and the speculations of Schelling and his friends. Microcosmic theories were also involved in the masterpieces of Schleiermacher and Schopenhauer. Fechner developed an imposing speculation by the aid of arguments from analogy; he was more concrete than Schelling, but was fantastic in his panpsychism. Lotze, using the microcosmic terminology, but assigning it some meanings of his own, developed an elaborate philosophy of values, which attempted to

---

[1] Sec. 269.

[2] Sec. 270. The organismic theory of society is discussed in chapter V, below.

[3] *Cf. Principles of Ethics* (New York, 1897), secs. 370, ff.; *cf.* Coker, work cited in chapter V, pp. 136 ff.

[4] *Princ. of Sociol.*, sec. 222; Coker, *loc. cit.*

[5] *Variations in Animals and Plants* (N. Y., 1868), vol. II, p. 483.

[6] Huxley, "The Connection of the Biological Sciences with Medicine," *Nature*, vol XXIV, p. 346 (1881).

[7] *Evolution and Ethics* (New York, 1899), pp. 59, 83.

solve the problems of mechanism by dismissing them as negligible in importance. But the rise of the theory of evolution led to new estimates of this importance, although it did not lead to further development of the microcosmic theories on any comprehensive scale. As a result of Spencer's presuppositions, and Huxley's conclusions, and the fact that presently increasing specialization and improved methods vastly augmented the data to be interpreted, attention was turned from the problems raised by Fechner and Lotze, who remain the outstanding representatives of consistent and detailed attempts to indicate by means of the microcosmic conceptions the place of man in the universe.

Appendix—Microcosmic Theories in the Works of Swedenborg

The world which Swedenborg (1688–1772) described as having been seen in his visions was organized on a macrocosmic and microcosmic plan; "correspondences" were prominent throughout the system. The Lord, by celestial things, regulates spiritual things; by spiritual things, natural things; and by natural things, corporeal things. This constitutes "order"; when a man is regenerated he acquires a corresponding order and thus becomes an image of heaven (*Arcana cœlestia*, Eng. transl., New York, 1873, 10 vols; paragraph 911). Conversely, heaven is called the Grand (*Ibid.*, paragr. 2996), or the Greatest Man (911). It is also said that this name is given because all things in . . . heaven correspond to the Lord (3741); and that there is a correspondence, through heaven, between the Lord and man (3883). Every part of the human body has something heavenly—usually a "society" (of angels)—corresponding to it (2996, 3884, 4041, 4045, 4523, 4528, 6013). From these societies celestial and spiritual things "flow in with man" (3630); from the correspondences man's subsistence is derived (2998). The universal heaven is such that every one is, as it were, the center of all (3633). Each society is an image of the whole, "for what is unanimous is composed of such images of itself" (4625). Still, all situations in heaven are determined in respect to the human body, and it is known from the situation what the societies are, and to what province of man's organs and members they belong (3639). The varieties of the life of good and truth in heaven are "according to the reception of life from the Lord," and have a relation to each other which is similar to the relation of portions of man's body (3744). Correspondence with the celestial makes man "principled in love to the Lord"; correspondence with the spiritual gives man charity for his neighbor (3634–3635). As to his spirit, man is, then, in heaven; as to his body he is in the world (3634–3635), and is formed "an image of the world" (6013). The internal man is a "heaven in the least form," and the external man is a "world in the least form," and thus a microcosm (6057). Material substances "correspond" as do heavenly substances, but in an inferior degree (3741). The whole body is an organ composed of the most concealed things of all that are in the nature of the world and according to their secret powers of acting and wonderful modes of flowing; this—which would now be called adaptation—is said to have been the reason why the ancients called man a microcosm (4523, 6057). The heart corresponds to the celestial, the lungs to the spiritual kingdom (3635). At death man goes into that society of whose general form he is an individual effigy (*The True Christian Religion*, Eng. transl., New York, 1872, paragraph 739).

## CHAPTER V

## TRACES OF MICROCOSMIC THEORIES IN RECENT SCIENCE AND PHILOSOPHY

### 1. Recent Microcosmic Theories Isolated and Scattered

During the past fifty years the sciences have progressed so rapidly and in such divergent directions that no attempts at synthesis comparable to that of Spencer have been made. In philosophy the Neo-Hegelians have abandoned the "Naturphilosophie," and the newer schools which have opposed them have been in great measure absorbed in problems of method. While theories corresponding to one or another of the older microcosmic theories have appeared, they have either been isolated in the midst of other doctrines, or they have consisted of vague generalizations or allusions. It is, however, worthy of note that in the great scientific advance all the principal sciences have made some use of theories to the effect that certain portions of the universe imitate certain others in structures and processes. A number of these microcosmic conceptions have been adopted only to be discredited later on; but for all that, new microcosmic conceptions keep appearing, and are even somewhat prominent in the sciences of the present day. We shall consider in this connection first, the so-called recapitulation theory in biology; second, the recapitulation theory in psychology, including the "culture-epoch" theory; third, the organismic theories of society and the state; fourth, microcosmic analogies employed in contemporary science; and fifth, microcosmic theories in recent and contemporary philosophy.

### 2. The Theory of Recapitulation in Biology

*1. Definition.* The recapitulation theory in biology asserts that an individual of a given species passes through successive stages of development, each of which represents a stage in the evolution of the species or of several successive species. Other terms for this view are "the morpho-genetic theory," "the biogenetic law," "the doctrine of parallelism," and "the repetition theory." [1]

---

[1] Davidson, cited below, p. 2.

*2. Early History of the Theory.*   The whole theory has been reviewed by P. E. Davidson, in his dissertation on *The Recapitulation Theory and Human Infancy*,[1] from which work the material for this section is almost entirely drawn.   Without attempting to do more than summarize what Davidson presents in detail, we may note that the beginnings of the recapitulation theory go back at least to Lorenz Oken, as noted above. K. E. Von Baer, whose name has sometimes been linked with the theory, introduced a very important modification when he stated, in 1828, that the resemblance between a mammalian embryo and other animal types was between corresponding embryonic stages, and not between the embryonic form of the mammal and the adult form of the other animals. L. Agassiz in 1857 elaborated a threefold parallelism between the geological succession of animals, their structural gradations, and the development of individual representatives.   E. Hæckel in 1866, in disregard of all doubtful cases and perhaps not without some inconsistency, gave the theory its popular formulation, to the effect that ontogeny recapitulates phylogeny.   In the same year A. Hyatt, in formulating his "law of acceleration" stated that modifications tend to be inherited at earlier and earlier stages, until they become embryonic; but E. D. Cope declared that acceleration did not operate uniformly, and that hence the recapitulation theory was inexact.[2]

*3. Differences of Opinion Among Authorities Since 1866.*   Among the large number of views of authorities in biology and paleontology assembled by Davidson one finds wide variations of opinion concerning the theory of recapitulation.   The theory is accepted by A. Dendy practically in the sense given it by Hæckel; Dendy says that however much modified it may be by abbreviation and the superposition of secondary features, the life-history of the individual is essentially a condensed epitome of the ancestral history of the race.[3]   W. E. Kellicott says something similar:

> "Repetition is seldom particular, or detailed, never complete, yet so many of the phenomena of development can be satisfactorily interpreted from the historical point of view, seeming to have this historical sign rather than an immediately adaptive relation, that as a general statement the law remains fundamentally true." [4]

[1] Teachers College, New York, 1914.

[2] *Ibid.*, pp. 5–28.

[3] *Outlines of Evolutionary Biology* (1912), p. 281; quoted by Davidson, p. 51. *Cf.* Dendy, pp. 265–267; Davidson, pp. 37–38.

[4] *Text-book of General Embryology* (1913), p. 24; quoted by Davidson, p. 52.

C. Deperet maintains that, if we consider only the most general features, it is indisputable that the development of an individual is a kind of rapid recapitulation of the slow phases of the evolution of the species and the branch; [1] but he also says that examples in fossil adult species of representation of the embryonic or youthful characteristics of existing animals cannot be generalized—they remain in the state of exceptional facts.[2] Other writers, among them K. von Zittel [3] and L. C. Miall,[4] have placed more emphasis upon the fact that the evidence is not complete. Still others have thought that after allowances have been made for the work of other agencies, something remains which may be called recapitulation, but have implied that it is not important; thus Hatschek and O. Hertwig have held that the egg cell of the developed organism and the amœba are comparable only in so far as they fall under the common definition of the cell; and that the two correspond not according to their contents, but only as to their form.[5] J. C. Ewart thought that while there were some remote resemblances between embryos and supposed ancestors, still there should be a limit to the use of the word recapitulation.[6] J. T. Cunningham held that in the case of the larva of the frog there was much more of adaptation than recapitulation.[7] Another group of investigators has attempted to restate the theory in terms of resemblances between present ontogeny and ancestral ontogeny; most prominent among them is T. H. Morgan who points out that in certain large groups, some forms develop in very different ways from others; that it is entirely arbitrary to assume that the group characters are the first to appear, and then successively those of the order, family, genus and species; that the early embryos of a group are not identical throughout different species; that it is absurd to claim that the ancestral adult condition is repeated when rudiments only appear; that cases of repetition of adult ancestral stages outside the group of vertebrates are often doubtful, sometimes little less than fanciful; and that embryos are to be compared not to ancestral adult forms but to ancestral embryos.[8]

[1] *Transformations of the Animal World* (Eng. transl., 1909), p. 254; quoted by Davidson, p. 17 n.

[2] *Ibid.*, Deperet, pp. 254–256; Davidson, pp. 32–33.

[3] *Natural Science*, VI, 308–309 (1895); Davidson, pp. 29–30.

[4] *Report of British Association . . . 1897*, p. 682; Davidson, p. 41 n.

[5] T. H. Morgan, *Evolution and Adaptation* (1903), pp. 78–83; Davidson, pp. 43–44.

[6] *Jour. Anat. and Physiol.*, XXVIII, pp. 348–350 (1893–4); Davidson, pp. 31–32.

[7] *Science Progress*, VI (1897), p. 489; Davidson, pp. 56–57.

[8] *Evolution and Adaptation*, pp. 73, 83; Davidson, pp. 52–54.

Finally, some writers have virtually abandoned the theory; T. H. Montgomery on the ground that difference must not be estimated from visible data alone, but that differences in growth-energies and ultra-observational structural bases must be taken into account;[1] and A. Sedgwick, who thinks that

> "the view that embryonic development is essentially a recapitulation of ancestral history must be given up; it contains only a few references to ancestral history"

in the way of characteristics which have been lost by the adult and have been absorbed into the embryonic or larval stages.[2] These divergent opinions are enough to show that the position of the recapitulation theory in biology is not easy to determine, but that there are at least some formidable objections to the free acceptance of the older views.

### 3. THE THEORY OF RECAPITULATION IN PSYCHOLOGY

*1. Recapitulation and "Culture-Epoch" Theories.* Carried over into psychology, the theory of recapitulation asserts that the development of the individual mind exhibits a resumé of the development of mind throughout the evolutionary series. As a special case of this, there is the "culture-epoch" theory, to the effect that the mind of a human individual presents in its development a resumé of various ancestral stages in human civilization.

*2. Early History of these Theories.* Theories of recapitulation are foreshadowed in ancient works, beginning with Aristotle, as noted above, wherever attention is drawn to the fact that man contains in himself characteristics of the other animal species. The theory received its most complete expression in the work of G. J. Romanes, who worked out an elaborate parallelism between the biological and psychological development of the individual and the various members of an evolutionary series of living forms.[3] The comparison of stages of human individual development with stages of human history goes back at least to Augustine; there are more or less definite traces of it in Lessing, Herder,[4] Herbart, Comte, and Spencer.[5] The culture-epoch theory was formulated very

---

[1] *Analysis of Racial Descent in Animals* (1906), pp. 191–192; Davidson, pp. 44–45.

[2] Art., "Embryology," *Encyc. Brit.* (11th ed.), p. 323; Davidson, pp. 54–55.

[3] *Mental Evolution in Man* (1889), p. 5. *Cf.* Table, frontispiece.

[4] A. F. Chamberlain, *The Child: A Study in the Evolution of Man* (London, 1906), p. 55.

[5] G. E. Vincent, *The Social Mind and Education* (New York, 1897), pp. 71–75.

definitely and rigidly by T. Ziller, who attempted to systematize the educational process on this basis.[1]

3. *Later Opinions Concerning These Theories.*  In recent years the theories have been the subject of considerable discussion in psychology and pedagogy.  Their most notable adherent has been G. S. Hall, who has held that although the recapitulation theory has limitations and qualifications in biology, its psychogenetic applications have a method of their own, and that the child and the race are each keys to the other.[2] According to Hall, most of the non-volitional movements of infancy and childhood may be regarded as rudimentary impulses to do acts which in some pre-human stage were of great importance for life.[3]  In play, children rehearse the activities of our ancestors, repeating their life work in summative and adumbrated ways.[4]  Accelerations and retardations in the height and weight of individual children are traces of ancient periods in which the development of the race was accelerated and retarded.[5] The characteristics of children from the age of eight to twelve suggest the culmination of one stage of life, as if it thus represented what was once the age of maturity in some remote, perhaps pygmoid, stage of human evolution.[6]  Adolescence recapitulates a prehistoric period of storm and stress.[7]  Phyletic explanations "of all degrees of probability" are suggested throughout the work.[8]  Several other writers have worked out similar views,[9] but there have been numerous criticisms of them.  J. M. Baldwin, while he compares in some detail various stages of biological development in the race and psychological development in the individual,[10] emphasizes the facts that habit and association,[11] accommodation,[12] and individual variation [13] may lead to short cuts or breaks.  J. Dewey says that while educational theory is indebted to the culture-epoch theory for the first systematic attempts to base a course of study upon the actual unfolding of child nature, certain important qualifications must be made; as usually stated, the doctrine underestimates processes and exaggerates the importance of products, and in applying the doctrine, the present and

---

[1] G. E. Vincent, *The Social Mind and Education* (New York, 1897), p. 81.

[2] *Adolescence* (New York, 1904), vol. I, p. viii.          [3] *Ibid.*, I, p. 160.

[4] *Ibid.*, I, 202.          [5] *Ibid.*, I, 48.

[6] *Ibid.*, I, pp. ix–x.          [7] *Ibid.*, I, p. xiii; II, 70, ff.

[8] *Ibid.*, I, p. viii; *cf.* I, 215–216, 264, 356, 366; II, 192–194, 212–219.

[9] See Vincent, *op. cit.*, pp. 76, ff.; Chamberlain, *op. cit.*, pp. 213, ff.; quotations in E. L. Thorndike, *Educational Psychology* (New York, 1913), vol. I, pp. 249, ff.

[10] *Mental Development in the Child and the Race* (New York, 1903), pp. 15–16.

[11] *Ibid.*, p. 20.          [12] *Ibid.*, p. 23.          [13] *Ibid.*, p. 32.

not the past should be accorded the primacy.[1]  P. E. Davidson thinks that psychological recapitulation varies from biological since in the former the stages remain functional throughout life, and the correspondence is less and less chronological.[2]  After a critique of other evidence offered for the theory, he concludes that in the case of intelligence, there may be a distinguishable progression in both series, although, as L. T. Hobhouse suggests, we are not yet in a position to state what is the real character of the correspondence, if it exists.[3]  E. A. Kirkpatrick emphasizes the importance of environmental action, and says that since in the nervous system the capacity for modification is greater than in any other part of the body, and since the environment affecting the development of the child is different from the environment of the race, there is little chance of parallel modifications; the child and the savage resemble each other chiefly because they are both, to a considerable extent, undeveloped intellectually, and because in both the highest nervous structures are only partially developed.  The order in which the different kinds of intelligence appear is doubtless the same—physiological, sensory-motor, representative, conceptual—but there can be a close parallel only when both have been in similar environments.[4]  G. A. Coe says that there is a considerable degree of similarity between child life and the "childhood of the race"; both the race and the individual show a movement of mind from immediate ends toward remote ones, from immediate data of sense toward thought structures of greater and greater complexity, from impulsiveness toward deliberation, and so on, but the individual must not be regarded as predetermined by his ancestral history, nor kept out of coöperative social enterprises until a supposedly "proper stage" is reached.[5]  Coe sketches, point by point, a contrast between the process of social education according to the recapitulation theory and the theory of continuity.[6]  Perhaps the most unfavorable view of recapitulation is that of Thorndike, who says of the biological theory that the clearest cases of recapitulation are those where the way taken to produce the structure is a likely way, apart from any tendency to recapitulate for

[1] Art., "Culture Epoch Theory," in P. Monroe's *Cyclopædia of Education* (New York, 1911), II, p. 241.

[2] *Op. cit.*, pp. 78–79.

[3] *Ibid.*, pp. 80–92; Hobhouse (*Mind in Evolution*, 1901, p. 327, n.), quoted on pp. 91–92.

[4] *Genetic Psychology* (New York, 1917), pp. 334, 357.

[5] *Social Theory of Religious Education* (New York, 1920), pp. 149–150.

[6] *Ibid.*, pp. 151–153.

recapitulation's sake. When it is admitted that distortions and omissions are frequent, little more is left of the theory than a useless general scheme for explaining facts whose existence has to be proved by direct observation. Of the psychological theory he says that it seems to be an attractive speculation with no more truth behind it than the fact that when a repetition of phylogeny, abbreviated and modified, is a useful way of producing an individual, the individual may be produced in that way. Thorndike thinks that no fact of value about either the ontogeny or the phylogeny of behavior has been discovered as a result of the recapitulation theory.[1] Thus it appears that the data for the psychological theories as well as for the biological theories of recapitulation are by no means clear, and that any attempt to construe microcosmic theories from them would find them as much of a liability as an asset.

### 4. Organismic Theories of Society and the State

*1. Early History of Organismic Theories.* Organismic theories of the state may be treated as a special case of the more general organismic theories of society. Comparisons, more or less metaphorical, between a society and an organism have been noted above in connection with Plato, John of Salisbury, Hobbes, Rousseau, and Spencer. A large number of other writers have been reviewed in this connection by O. Gierke in the work above noted. He thinks that mediæval thought proceeded from the idea of a single whole, under the influence of Biblical allegories and a continuous tradition of pictorial phrases "in classical writings," and that it was motivated by the desire that Church and State should complete each other.[2] During the Middle Ages the organic view promoted recognition of mutual obligations and even of necessary differences in rank, and of centralized control; but it was conceived in terms of creation more than of evolution, and failed to reach the conception of the state as a legal person.[3] Another large group of writers is considered by F. W. Coker in his monograph on *Organismic Theories of the State.*[4]

---

[1] *Educational Psychology* (New York, 1913), vol. I, pp. 254–258.

[2] *Op. cit.,* pp. 22–23, and note 77.

[3] Pp. 27–30. He cites as typical of the mediæval view, Dante, *De monarchia,* I, Chapters vi and vii.

[4] In Columbia University *Studies in History, Economics and Public Law,* vol. 38 (1910). This work is later than those of T. van Krieken and E. T. Towne (p. 6). Some of the minor writers mentioned as having held organismic theories are C. T. Welcker, who (1813) compared the ages of political development with the ages of an

The most important of the earlier writers, other than those mentioned above, was Comte. Coker says that the organismic character of Comte's interpretation of the nature of society and social forces appears from his frequent recourse to analogies between society and an organism. Society is called a social or collective organism, and has the organic attribute of a "universal consensus," or harmony of all structures and functions working toward a common end, and making government necessary.[1] "Social statics" corresponds to the anatomy, and "social dynamics" to

individual (pp. 47, ff.); J. von Görres, who (1819) compared the democratic and monarchic elements in a state to automatic and voluntary actions in man (pp. 44 ff.); K. S. Zacharia, who (1839–42) held that the state is, at least ideally, like an individual, a combination of spirit and matter, made up of units, with characteristics corresponding to those of plants, animals and men, and should maintain its life by action, vital integrity, unity, and inner efficiency (pp. 84, ff.); F. T. Rohmer, who (1844) held that the fundamental forces of the human soul develop in four life stages, which also explain the development of the state, so that boyhood parallels radicalism, youth liberalism, and so on (pp. 49, ff.); H. Ahrens, who (1850), although he was careful to specify that the state is not a natural organism, compared it to the nervous apparatus of volition in the individual, and explained the differences between state and organism by the presence of a knowing, valuing and selective activity in the case of the state, and by the fact that the state deals in ideal goods (pp. 32, ff.); K. Volgraff, who (1851–5) based his system upon the four cardinal human temperaments, distributing humanity into four races, each race into four classes, each class into four orders, and each order into four tribes, and compared the organization of an organism to the constitution or state-form, which is composed of four subordinate organisms—the civil, judicial, financial, and military, corresponding to physiological arrangements, processes which maintain health, nutritive system and protective system, respectively (pp. 60–62, 92–95); J. C. Planta, for whom (1852), a fundamental and universal system was polarity and mutual supplementation, and who thought the state exhibits such a living supplementation of the masculine-individualistic-subjective-rational and the feminine-universalistic-objective-emotional; that the state has a soul in the collective political consciousness, and organs, legislation constituting the heart and government the brain (p. 90, n.); and J. K. Bluntschli, who (1852–70) makes what is in some ways the most exaggerated application of the organismic conception of any of the political philosophers (p. 105). For Bluntschli the state is a living organism, not indeed a pure product of nature (p. 106), but a union of soul and body, with parts animated by special impulses and capacities (p. 107), with some parts subordinate to others (p. 110), developing from within outwards, possessed of an individuality (p. 107), and being mortal (p. 112). The state is preëminently a moral and spiritual organism (p. 112). It is masculine, compared to the church, which is characteristically feminine (p. 113, f.). It is the image of the human being, and also the image of man (p. 114).

[1] *Cours de philosophie positive* (4th ed., 1877), vol. IV, pp. 235–243; VI, 712, cited by Coker, p. 123.

the physiology of an organism.[1]  But the major portion of the latter
treats of the "law of the three stages," to the effect that human intelligence, in the individual as in the race, passes through the theological,
metaphysical, and positive stages [2]—all of which may be reckoned among
the theories of recapitulation rather than the organismic theories.  Organismic in its suggestion, if not in its actual presentation, is Comte's doctrine of Humanity as The Great Being in whom all participate.

2. *Bearing of Microcosmic Theories upon the Work of Lilienfeld.*  Contemporary of Spencer and perhaps uninfluenced by him,[3] P. von Lilienfeld was an important figure among the organicists.  His teachings have
been reviewed by both Barth and Coker; but neither has noted the bearing of microcosmic theories upon them.  Lilienfeld holds that throughout
all nature there is a tendency to concentration and individuation,[4]
evident in the formation of atoms, molecules, cells, organs, organisms,
and combinations of organisms.[5]  Every inorganic body in this way
exhibits in itself what the universe exhibits; both inorganic bodies [6] and
societies [7] may be compared to the solar system.  Every cell is a microcosm of the individual of which it forms a constituent part,[8] and every
individual is a microcosm of society.[9]  Lilienfeld held it to be an established result, not only in metaphysics, but also in science, that the universe exhibits in the large what man on a small scale contains within
himself, "in other words, that man and the physical world around him
are related to one another as a microcosm to a macrocosm."  That this
is really true he thinks is shown by the biological theory of recapitulation,
as well as by the fact that the human body exhibits the mechanical,
physical, and chemical processes of all bodies.  The higher social life of
man, too, is a microcosm of all human history; human society is a
"social cosmos"; this, says Lilienfeld, results from his introductory
considerations [10] in which society is held to be a "real organism."  These
correspondences and relations furnish a background and setting for

[1] Coker, p. 119.

[2] *Philos. positive,* IV, 490, cited by Coker, p. 120.

[3] P. Barth, *Die Philosophie der Geschichte als Sociologie* (Leipzig, 1897), pp. 127-128
and note.

[4] *Gedanken über die Socialwissenschaft der Zukunft* (Mitau, 1873, etc.), I, 114.

[5] *Ibid.,* I, 131-132; *cf.* II, 310.

[6] *Ibid.,* I, 130.      [7] *Ibid.,* I, 133.

[8] *La pathologie sociale* (Paris, 1896), p. 165.

[9] *Ibid.,* p. 166; *Gedanken,* II, p. 310.

[10] *Gedanken,* I, 280-281.

Lilienfeld's organismic sociology. He thinks that society exhibits the
five characteristic marks of an organism—intense and varied interaction
of forces, inner unity, purposiveness, differentiation, in the course of a
life-cycle, and capitalization, or the storing up of energies and materials
for future consumption.[1] This last is apparent in the universe as well
as in society.[2] Differences between a society and an organism are explained by the fact that society is an organism of a higher degree,[3] or that
the biological organisms have been subjected to different environmental
actions,[4] or that society is not a visible organism because we ourselves
form a part of it.[5] The social organism is made up of cells, or individuals,
and "inter-cellular substance," or the physical and economic environment.[6] The economic functions of a society, including production,
exchange, consumption, growth and reproduction, are or may be compared to the physiological functions of an organism;[7] the judicial
functions of a society may be compared to the morphological relations of
an organism, since they have to do with its divisions into parts; and the
political functions of a society, like the individuating principle of an
organism, make it a unity.[8] Political disturbances are compared to
diseases, and are traced to lack of purposive development,[9] lack of
harmony between whole and parts,[10] or to alterations in the place-,
time-, or mass-relations of constituent units.[11] Treatment may consist
in a process of excitation or depression, with changes of distribution,[12]
unless death, in the form of social disintegration,[13] intervenes. Lilienfeld
evidently felt the force of the objection which has since developed into
the psychological theory of society; for to think of society in terms of an
organism seems to reduce it to the vegetative level, and not to do justice
to human achievements. He attempts to meet this by the view that a
society is a combination of nerve-cells rather than a combination of cells
in the more general sense;[14] a society has no muscular system or osseous
structure.[15] This has been interpreted by Barth[16] and Coker[17] to mean
that the nervous systems of individual men, as distinct from the rest of
their bodies, form the constituent "cells" of the social organism; but it

[1] *Gedanken*, I, 55–68.     [2] *Ibid.*, I, 295.     [3] *Ibid.*, I, 51–52, 80.
[4] *Ibid.*, I, 89–91.     [5] *Ibid.*, I, 143, 150.     [6] *Ibid.*, I, 176–177.
[7] *Pathologie*, p. xxix; *Gedanken*, I, 81–82, 152–153.     [8] *Gedanken*, I, 87.
[9] *Ibid.*, I, 167.     [10] *Ibid.*, I, 170.
[11] *Pathologie*, pt. II, chaps. IV, ff.; Coker, *op. cit.*, p. 152.
[12] *Pathologie*, p. 230.     [13] *Gedanken*, I, 158.     [14] *Ibid.*, I, 139.
[15] *Pathologie*, p. 227; *cf. Ann. de l'Inst. de sociol.*, IV, 226.
[16] *Op. cit.*, pp. 129–130.     [17] *Op. cit.*, p. 145.

seems to be more accurate, and more in accord with what we have called
the macrocosmic setting of Lilienfeld's sociology, to say that at least
sometimes his view is that the individuals of a society are related to their
environment as the cells of a nervous system are related to their inter-
cellular substance, but that a man in the environment constitutes, since
he has his entire nervous system, a much more highly developed "nervous cell" than any of those which he as a biological individual contains.[1]
This would make society an organ of the environment rather than,
strictly speaking, an organism; but Lilienfeld holds that the terms
"organic system" and "organism" are identical.[2]

3. *Organismic Theories of Other Writers.* A. Schaeffle, in his elaborate
*Bau und Leben des Socialen Körpers*,[3] carried the analogies of Spencer and
Lilienfeld farther, but omitted some of them in his second edition,[4] in
which he emphasized the fact that society, compared with an organism,
presents characteristics which are unique.[5] He intended to avoid the
term "organism,"[6] but used the term "organ" in connection with the
"social body,"[7] and analyzed the latter in terms of morphology, physiology, and psychology.[8] The social cell, or unit, is the family,[9] which is
"the primitive social microcosm";[10] accordingly there is both inter-
cellular and intracellular substance, the latter being the private property
of the family.[11] Although the origin of social arrangements is said to be
spiritual, there is an elaborate doctrine of social tissues.[12] To family
relationships in general corresponds the connective tissue of organisms;[13]
to the protective arrangements of society correspond epidermal tissues
and the like;[14] to the economic processes of society correspond the
nutritive and circulatory processes of an organism;[15] to the technical
establishments of society correspond the muscular tissues;[16] and to
intelligently directed human social life, comprising individual nervous
systems and the symbols, linguistic, artistic, etc., which these employ,
corresponds the nervous tissue, with its nerve cells and fibres.[17] Schaeffle
develops the last-named analogy at considerable length—great cities

[1] Lilienfeld says as much, *Gedanken*, I, 178.        [2] *Ibid.*, I, 150.
[3] 1st ed., 1875–1878; citations here are from reprint of 2nd ed., Tübingen, 1896.
[4] Vol. I, p. iv.        [5] I, pp. iv, v.        [6] I, pp. vii, 18.        [7] I, 138.        [8] I, p. ix.
[9] I, 18, 20, 26, 66, 106.        [10] I, 76.        [11] I, 20, 69.
[12] I, 86, 104 ff. Barth (*op. cit.*, p. 141) says that Schaeffle has no analogy for social
"domiciliation"; but Schaeffle thought that the fact that organisms and society had
the same environment made other analogies inevitable (I, p. iv).
[13] I, 21, 67, 109.        [14] I, 112.        [15] I, 31, 79, 112.
[16] I, 21, 117 ff.        [17] I, 124.

correspond to the higher nervous centers, provincial towns to the spinal column, outlying districts to the peripheral nerves; [1] the civilized arrangements for the distribution of commodities are analogous to the nervous integration of the viscera; [2] a society even obeys Fechner's law and the law of summation.[3] Just as the central nervous system sometimes intervenes in the activity of an organism, otherwise reflex, so a government must sometimes intervene in society, but neither absolute centralization nor absolute decentralization is normal.[4] A. Fouillée, in his *La science sociale contemporaine*,[5] tried to reconcile opposing theories of society by calling society a "contractual organism." [6] There are, he thinks, three kinds of organisms—those of the lower animals, in which consciousness is confused and dispersed; those of the higher animals, in which consciousness is clear and concentrated; and those of societies, in which consciousness is clear and dispersed.[7] There is nothing in society analogous to the concentration of self-consciousness in the case of an individual; [8] but the thinkers and leaders among men are analogous to the most highly developed brain cells in an organism.[9] The organismic theory has among its political implications an emphasis upon the mutual dependence of the parts of a state, the dangers of brusque reforms, the superiority of evolution to revolution—although the latter may sometimes be necessary—and the reconciliation of progressive and conservative doctrines in a liberalism which will provide for both autonomy and centralization.[10] One must remember that in a society, factors of intelligence and will are involved; [11] in fact, a society is an organism because it is thought, and wished.[12] Fouillée goes on to attempt a higher synthesis; for the universe, too, with its reciprocal actions and reactions is like a vast organism; and it may be supposed to be an organism which is social, or tends to become social, conscious and volitional. That which man knows as will may be taken to be the principle of the universe, which was only vague in the early stages of evolution, but later on becomes clear. Society may in this sense be said to be the end of the universe; "if the individual organism is already a little world, society is still more worthy of the name of microcosm." [13] Moreover, language,

---

[1] I, 135.    [2] I, 136.    [3] I, 179, 180.    [4] I, 23, 137.

[5] 1st ed., 1880; citations here from 2nd ed., Paris, 1885. On Fouillée, see Coker, pp. 180 ff.

[6] *La science sociale*, pp. 111, ff.    [7] *Ibid.*, pp. 245–246.

[8] *Ibid.*, p. 243.    [9] *Ibid.*, p. 108.

[10] *Ibid.*, pp. 128 ff.    [11] *Ibid.*, pp. 143–144.    [12] *Ibid.*, p. 115.

[13] *Ibid.*, pp. 411–415; *cf.* pp. 123–127.

which develops naturally in society, is a whole world, an image of the world of thought, and of the universe. Perhaps then the universe is a society of beings whose members coöperate, at first unconsciously, but later reflectively, in the life of the whole.[1] W. Wundt, in his *System der Philosophie* had a word to say for the organismic theories; that, although many saw in them only metaphors, still the differences between societies and organisms should not hide the fundamental fact that such binding into a unified whole, with division into organs between which there is division of labor, has the characteristic marks of an organism; but the fact that the individuals of a society can form an idea of their own spiritual nature forbids any further analogy.[2] Apart from such considerations, individuals and societies are bound by relations of collective consciousness and collective personality.[3] J. S. Mackenzie, in his *Introduction to Social Philosophy*,[4] held that an organism is a little universe in itself; it is a universe, and not a unit—it has parts, it grows, and has an end.[5] In these respects, society is more nearly analogous to an organic whole than to any other type of unity;[6] but since the end of society is the highest life of its individual members, it need be called organic, if at all, only in the sense that it is an incomplete whole, whose completion would consist simply in its own perfect development.[7]

R. Worms, in his *Organisme et société*, worked out one of the most definite and thorough parallelisms between the two, comparing their anatomy, physiology, and pathology in detail.[8] He presents some answers to objections that have been raised against the organismic theories, especially by Fouillée. To the objection that "only individuals exist," Worms replies that biology shows all individuation to be relative.[9] To the objection that cells cannot live freely in an organism as individuals can in society, he says that sometimes cells live when separated from their parent organisms, and that, on the other hand, individuals in society are interdependent.[10] To the objection that the biological organisms are continuous in structure, with contiguous parts, he says that society has everything that contiguity secures for the organism, namely, inner continuity of movement and interchange of utilities, and that

---

[1] *La science sociale*, pp. 416–417.
[2] Wundt, *System* (Leipzig, 1889), pp. 598, ff.
[3] *Ibid.*, pp. 600, ff.     [4] New York, 1895.     [5] P. 164.     [6] P. 176.
[7] Pp. 272–273.
[8] Worms, *Org. et soc.* (Paris, 1896), p. 7. See Coker, *op. cit.*, pp. 170 ff.
[9] Worms, *op. cit.*, p. 42.     [10] *Ibid.*, pp. 46–51.

moreover there is no actual contact of vital parts either in plant or ani-mal.[1]  To the objection that in the biological organism consciousness is concentrated, while in a society it is diffuse, he replies that the distinc-tion is not absolute; a great part of man's activity is unconscious, and cells not in the nervous system must be supposed to have some rudi-mentary consciousness.[2]  At the time same, the resemblances between organisms and societies must not be construed as identities, and some of the relative differences between them are important.[3]  Consideration of them leads to the view that a society is a super-organism, an organism with added features.[4]  In a later discussion, Worms says that, although the organismic method is not the only method to be used in sociology, it can reconcile psychological theories of society and the view of economic materialism,[5] and that it shows the error both of radical individualism and of utopian socialism.[6]  J. Novicow, in his *Conscience et volonté sociale* says that a society differs from an organism in its morphology; most civilized societies resemble an embryonic nervous system more than they resemble man—but the biological resemblances are complete.[7] The cell, "already a world," goes on to form the higher aggregate of the organic individual; there is nothing to prevent a still higher aggregate of these individuals.[8]  To the objection that in a society an individual can form a part of more than one institution or group, whereas in an organism a cell can form a part of only one organ, Novicow replies that an organ may exercise different functions, although not at the same time; and, again, that the difference is one of degree—just as living substances are more unstable than non-living chemical compounds, so societies, the next higher aggregate, are more unstable than living substances.[9]  To the objection that the constituent cells of an organism have no individual consciousness analogous to that which is found in the members of a society, he says that the members of a society are conscious each of his individual life, but not of the life of the group, so that the analogy holds, after all.[10]  Those individuals who are most vividly conscious constitute the social sensorium; the social organ analogous to the brain is not the

[1] Worms, *op cit.*, pp. 51–53.
[2] *Ibid.*, p. 59.      [3] *Ibid.*, pp. 72, ff.      [4] *Ibid.*, pp. 9, 394.
[5] *Ann. de l'Inst. de sociol.*, IV, p. 303 (1898); Coker, *op. cit.*, p. 179.
[6] *Ibid.*, *Ann.*, pp. 296–304; Coker, pp. 178–9.
[7] Novicow, *Conscience* . . . . (Paris, 1897), pp. 9, 100.
[8] *Ann. de l'Inst. de sociol.*, IV, 188.
[9] *Ibid.*, IV, 182–183.
[10] *Conscience*, p. 19.

government, but the "social élite."[1]  In this group, as in the brain's process of volition, a project rallies its supporters.[2]  The history of a society is analogous to the memory of an individual.[3]  Novicow's general conclusion is that societies are organisms of a particular nature.[4]  Without the organic theory, he thinks that sociology would be either purely empirical or hopelessly metaphysical.[5]

4. *Critique of the Organismic Theories.*  It is well known that the objections[6] to the organismic theories of society and the state have proved too strong for them, and have reduced them to the status of suggestive metaphors or partial truths.[7]  Even where the analogies could be defended—and the arguments brought against them were sometimes the more faulty of the two—the logical and metaphysical objections[8] to their use have remained formidable, and the practical consequences as drawn from them have not been impressive.[9]  The great objection is that the organicists, in spite of their varied efforts, have been too abstract, and have not made adequate provision for the facts of human intelligence, and the higher life of man.  Yet it may be worth noting that the failure, as well as the rise, of the organismic theories occurs in the period of the decline of microcosmic theories in general.[10]  Lilienfeld and Fouillée, at least, argued for the existence of an organismic society in what they deemed to be an appropriate cosmic setting; but so little help in this direction has been forthcoming from any other quarter of philosophy[11] that the issues raised by the organismic theories have been decided upon quite other grounds.

---

[1] *Conscience*, pp. 19–20; *cf.* p. 220.        [2] *Ibid.*, p. 113.

[3] *Ibid.*, p. 33.        [4] *Ann. de l'Inst. de soc.*, IV, 183.

[5] *Ibid.*, pp. 188–191.  L. Gumplowicz, in his *Geschichte der Staatstheorien* (Innsbruck, 1905), p. 437, compares the world of the natural sciences, the macrocosm, with "the social-political microcosm," maintaining that the doctrine of a supreme miracle-worker is erroneous in the latter as in the former.

[6] For refs., Coker, *op. cit.*, p. 209.

[7] *Cf.* F. H. Giddings, *Principles of Sociology* (New York, 1911), p. 420; C. A. Ellwood, *Sociology in Its Psychological Aspects* (New York, 1912), pp. 386 ff.

[8] *E. g.*, Barth, *op. cit.*, pp. 93, 164; Coker, *op. cit.*, pp. 198 ff.

[9] Coker, p. 201.

[10] The microcosmic affiliations of the organismic theories have been urged as an argument against them.    L. Stein (*Ann. de l'Inst. de sociol.*, vol. IV, p. 289) said that organismic views marked a recurrence to a primitive anthropomorphism akin to that of the Pythagoreans, except that it is not the universe, but the social group, which is regarded as the macrocosm.

[11] *Cf.* the work of Renouvier, Royce, and Spaulding, cited in section 6.

## 5. MICROCOSMIC ANALOGIES EMPLOYED IN CONTEMPORARY SCIENCE

*1. Possible Implications of Current Analogies.* In spite of the fact that such microcosmic views as are implied in the theories of recapitulation and the organismic theories of society have been subjected to serious criticisms, one finds that at the present time the various sciences frequently draw upon one another for illustrative analogies which, if they are to be taken seriously, imply that structures and processes of portions of the universe which vary in size resemble one another, and that relations which may be termed microcosmic obtain between them. This implication is not always developed; and it may be said in general that the possible significance of the analogies presented is not investigated. Some of the analogies which have recently been used are indicated in the following paragraphs.

*2. Analogies between Structures Studied in Physics, Chemistry, and Astronomy.* P. Kropotkin in 1893 declared that chemistry was gradually introducing the idea of mass and motion into its symbols and considering the molecule as a system of minute bodies oscillating around a common center, comparable to a system of stars, and constituting "a particle of the universe on a microscopic scale—a microcosmos which lives the same life." [1]   Recent work on the structure of atoms has led to the view that all the chemical elements are made up of positively charged cores or nuclei, surrounded by orbital electrons.[2]   There have been some notable criticisms of the view,[3] and many points remain to be worked out before it can be accepted without qualification, but on the whole the alleged analogy between an atom and a solar system has come to be familiar. A. D. Cole has called such an atom "a world in itself" and a "complex microcosm"; [4] and E. Fournier d'Albé has gone so far as to say that we may even imagine the electron to be "a veritable microcosm." [5]   The last-named writer has also worked out what he holds to be a geometrical

[1] "Recent Science," *Nineteenth Century*, vol. XXXIV, p. 252 (1893). The molecule is called a microcosm by Benjamin Moore in a popular work, *The Origin and Nature of Life* (New York, 1913?), p. 105; *cf.* p. 79.

[2] See, *e. g.*, E. Rutherford, "On the Structure of the Atom," *Philosophical Magazine* (6), vol. XXVII, pp. 488, ff.

[3] See, *e. g.*, I. Langmuir, "The Arrangement of Electrons in Atoms and Molecules," *Journal of the American Chemical Society*, vol. XLI (1), pp. 868, ff. (1919); esp., pp. 931–932.

[4] "Recent Evidence for the Existence of the Nucleus Atom," *Science*, N. S., vol. XLI, p. 73 (1915).

[5] *The Electron Theory* (London, 1909), pp. 288–289.

ratio between the dimensions of an electron, the earth, and the galaxy—a ratio of approximately ten thousand trillions to one, which he thinks is "nothing less than the ratio of the scales of successive universes." [1] He finds in the "fruitful and suggestive astronomico-chemical analogy a boundless vista of worlds within worlds." [2] However this may be, one can at least take as significant the statement of W. D. McMillan:

> "We find ourselves almost midway in a series of physical units. On the one side we have the electrons, atoms and molecules, and on the other we have the ordinary masses, stars and galaxies. . . . Each physical unit is analyzed into units of the next lower order and synthesized into those of the next higher order. Each unit is an organization endowed with the proper amount of energy to carry on its existence and to insure its identity." [3]

*3. Attempts to Interpret Astronomy in Terms of Biology.* In recent years there have been attempts, more or less metaphorical, to understand astronomy in terms of biology. A. W. Bickerton has worked out a theory of the origin of new stars from "grazing impacts" of older stars; his title is *The Birth of Worlds and Systems*.[4] T. C. Chamberlin, using a series of biological metaphors, thinks that our "planetary system must clearly have had a bi-parental origin"; that while collision, "a bi-parental process . . . has stood in a parental relation to new celestial evolutions,[5]" our system arose from the near approach of a passing star to the sun, with attendant disturbances which gave rise to the solar nebula and planetary knots.[6] Percival Lowell once referred to the solar system as "an articulated whole, an inorganic organism, which not only evolved, but evolved in a definite order." [7] Fournier d'Albé has taken such resemblances more seriously:

> "The question of the possible life of the galactic system as an organism may at first sight appear strange or even absurd; but can we logically deny it or make it improbable? Reduce spaces and times by the world-ratio, and we have atoms in rapid motion . . . with an inner nucleus and outer rim or cell-wall sufficiently cohesive to

---

[1] *Two New Worlds* (London, 1907), pp. 9–10.

[2] *Electron Theory*, p. 290.

[3] " The Structure of the Universe," *Science*, N. S., LII, p. 67 (1920).

[4] London, 1911.

[5] *The Origin of the Earth* (Chicago, 1916), pp. 101–102.

[6] *Ibid.*, pp. 130, 135.

[7] Quoted in *Nature*, vol. XCI, p. 539 (1913).

exhibit individuality, but sufficiently open to admit material from outside. . . . We should be chary of denying every species of life to an aggregation of matter simply because it is very bulky and its evolution is difficult to observe." [1]

*4. Attempts to Interpret Geology in Terms of Anatomy and Physiology.* Ancient views to the effect that the earth is a living creature have some curious points of resemblance with recent geology. S. Meunier, in his *Les harmonies de l'évolution terrestre*, compared the earth's structure to an anatomy, and declared that the earth resembled "d'une manière troublante" a gigantic organism.[2] He mentioned particularly the mechanisms of transformation and displacement, which make possible the circulatory processes which keep the earth in equilibrium.[3] He has elaborated this view in a later work, *La géologie biologique.*[4] The work of Chamberlin, mentioned above, contains some striking metaphors drawn from the field of physiology. The planetesimals were the food on which the planetary knots fed;[5] the spacing of planets was modified by the character of their "feeding-ground."[6] Even statements which are not meant metaphorically suggest more or less close resemblance to anatomy, as when it is said that the earth developed a segmented structure, with certain great gyrals over the ocean, through which the superior accessions of planetesimal dust were received.[7] Chamberlin says that the function of igneous effusion in the economy of the earth may be likened to that of perspiration in the case of an animal.[8]

*5. The Views of A. J. Herbertson.* In recent years there has been one suggestion of the relation between biology and geology which lies along the line of the speculations of Fechner, Fourier, Lilienfeld, and Fouillée. A. J. Herbertson, at the British Association meeting in 1913, spoke of any one of what he called the "natural regions" of the earth as "a symbiotic association of plants, animals, men, indissolubly bound up with certain structures and forms of the land, possessing a definite water circulation, and subjected to a seasonal climactic rhythm,"[9] and said that "man in the natural region may be compared with nerve cells in an animal."[10] The fact that such regional units are complex he declared to

---

[1] *Two New Worlds*, pp. 126–127.
[2] Paris, 1908, p. 16.    [3] *Ibid.*, p. 19.    [4] Paris, 1914. See esp., p. 301.
[5] *The Origin of the Earth*, p. 141.
[6] *Ibid.*, p. 152.    [7] *Ibid.*, pp. 195–198.    [8] *Ibid.*, pp. 239–240.
[9] *Report of the British Association for the Advancement of Science*, 1913, p. 557.
[10] *Ibid.*, p. 559.

be "no reason for not applying scientific methods to their investigation, nor for doubting that substantial results can be gained by their use." [1] In an article in *Scientia* in the same year he said that the term macro-organism might be given to such a complex entity.

"If these geographical regions and localities are taken as representing organs, tissues and cells, we perhaps get nearest to a useful comparison—but such comparison is not essential and need not be pressed. . . . Such regional leviathans exist, and we are each a part of them. If the geographical region is a macro-organism, then men are its nerve-cells. . . . Man is no more, though no less, to be considered apart from the rest of these leviathans than the nervous system is to be considered apart from the rest of the organism of which it is an essential element." [2]

*6. Attempts to Interpret Biology in Terms of Sociology.* Parallelisms recalling the organismic theories of society are sometimes found in connection with biology. According to H. E. Crampton, in describing certain metazoa

"it is absolutely necessary to employ the terms of human social organization, because the hydra's body is a true colony of diverse cells in exactly the same sense that a nation is a body of human beings with more or less dissimilar social functions. To begin with the differentiation into ectoderm and endoderm, the organism is comparable to a human community made up of military and agricultural classes." [3]

C. S. Sherrington also has linked the two fields:

"The old Greek simile of our school classic likened man's body to the body politic . . . a corporate whole composed of individual members. Biology gives this a literal truth. The microscope reveals that plants and animals are literally commonwealths of individually living units. . . . Thus the corporeal house of life is built of living stones. In that house each stone is a self-centred microcosm. . . ." [4]

In this connection it may be noted that Sherrington elsewhere calls the organism a microcosm.[5]

[1] *Report of the British Association for the Advancement of Science,* 1913, p. 557.
[2] "The Higher Units," *Scientia,* vol. XIV, pp. 205, 212 (1913).
[3] *The Doctrine of Evolution* (New York, 1911), p. 255. *Cf.* pp. 20–21.
[4] "Physiology; Its Scope and Method" in *Lectures on the Method of Science,* ed. by T. B. Strong (Oxford, 1906), p. 67.
[5] *The Integrative Action of the Nervous System* (New Haven, 1906), p. 160.

*7. Attempts to Interpret Psychology in Terms of Biology.*[1] Thorndike has suggested some points of resemblance between psychology and biology:

"We should look upon the mental life of an individual as developing in the same way that the animal or plant kingdom has developed. As conditions of heat and food supply have everywhere been the first requisite to and influence on animal life, so the physiological conditions of the brain's activities are the first modifiers of feeling and action. As the stimuli of climate, food, . . . and the rest have . . . rendered possible the production of millions of different animal types, so the sights and sounds and smells of things . . . awaken in the mind new mental varieties, new species of thoughts and acts. In a score of years from birth the human mind, like the animal world, originates its universe of mental forms. As in the animal kingdom, many of these variations fail to fit the conditions . . . and die . . . so many of the mental forms produced are doomed to a speedy disappearance in consequence of their failure to fit outside events. The elimination of one species by others in the animal world is again paralleled by the death of those thoughts or acts which are out of harmony with others. Species of thoughts, like species of animals, prey upon one another, in a struggle in which survival is the victor's reward. Just as species of animals fitted to one environment perish or become transformed when that environment changes, so mental forms fitted to infancy perish or are transformed . . . throughout the incessant changes of a mind's surroundings. . . . The condition of a man's mind at any stage in its history is then, like the condition of the animal kingdom at any stage in the history of the world, the result not only of the new varieties which have appeared, but also of a natural selection working upon them."[2]

W. P. Montague in his *Variation, Heredity and Consciousness* says that the brain "builds up a 'psychic organism,' a life within a life, composed of differentiated forms of energy."[3]

*8. Attempts to Interpret Logic in Terms of Biology.* Finally there may be mentioned a tendency to import biological comparisons into logic. B. Bosanquet in the preface to his *Logic*, the sub-title of which is *The Morphology of Knowledge*, writes that he is indebted to Alfred Robinson

[1] See work of Herbart, cited above, and Royce, below.
[2] *Educational Psychology*, III, pp. 308–309.
[3] *Proc. Aristotelian Society*, vol. XXI, p. 39 (1921).

for the suggestion of a comparison between the study and analysis of judgment forms and the study and analysis of the forms of flowers and plants.

"... I have never seemed to myself able to exhaust its suggestiveness. If I have at all reproduced for others the spectacle of continuity and unity in the intellectual life, combined with the most varied and precise adaptation of its fundamentally identical function to manifold conditions and purposes, which this comparison never fails to present to my own mind, I shall so far have succeeded in the object of my work." [1]

He says that it is essential for this view that the form of thought be regarded as a living function, and that therefore the "morphology of knowledge" be construed as not excluding the "physiology of thought." [2] According to J. E. Creighton, the thought by which modern logic is dominated is that of the unity and continuity of all intellectual life.

"Thought is regarded as an organic, living function or activity, which remains identical with itself throughout all its developing forms and phases. . . . The conception of an organism whose parts are developing in mutual relation and interdependence promises to be as fruitful when applied to logic as it has already shown itself to be in other sciences." [3]

Creighton thinks that the evolutionary concepts of change, differentiation of structure, specialization and integration apply also to thinking,[4] but that such application may sometime come to be recognized as weak.[5]

## 6. MICROCOSMIC THEORIES IN RECENT AND CONTEMPORARY PHILOSOPHY

*1. General Characteristics of this Period.* That the philosophies of the present day are more diversified than those of other periods is partly true, as a consequence of the broadening of the field of knowledge and the diversity of facts to be considered; but it is partly an illusion, due to the fact that in estimating the present we lack the perspective which has toned down so many of the diversities of the past. Among writers whose works are now current one finds numerous differences of opinion regarding the microcosmic theories; the remarkable fact is that the terminology and

[1] B. Bosanquet, *Logic* (Oxford, 1888), p. vii.
[2] *Ibid.*, p. 2.
[3] *An Introductory Logic* (New York, 1920), pp. 34–35.
[4] *Ibid.*, p. 317, ff.
[5] *Ibid.*, p. 314.

so much of the content of the theories are retained by men who differ widely at other points. Some of the writers whom we shall consider, for example Paulsen and Renouvier, offer more or less explicit restatements of older views; while other writers, although never entirely independent of older views, make individual contributions which are more noteworthy.

*2. Paulsen's Restatement of Fechner.*    F. Paulsen followed Fechner in matters which concern the microcosmic theories, adding here and there a word about the method—that it ought to show that the astrophysical estimate of the planets is not the last nor the only one possible,[1] and that it ought to reconcile science and religion—for while it is not strictly scientific, still, whoever follows the indications of things attentively and gets an unspoiled impression of reality will be led ultimately to such ideas. In this philosophy, too, the fact of life becomes interpretable, in its origin, and place in the totality of things.[2]

*3. The "Nouvelle Monadologie" of Renouvier and Prat.*    A combination of Leibnitzian monadism with Kantian phenomenalism is presented by C. Renouvier and L. Prat. Molecules and atoms are to be regarded as physical abstractions.[3] Monads are metaphysical, and differ from atoms in that the latter possess no representative faculties;[4] the monad is a simple substance, reduced to essential relations of being.[5] The monads, however, form by their groupings the molecules of simple inorganic bodies.[6] A living organism is a functional organization of monads; each of its subordinate organs may be a functional organization, and may be said to be living. The central or directing monad of each organism is set over its little world, and may be said to be living in an eminent degree.[7] Each organism, and in the organism, each organ, is a society; but a society is not an organism, because individuals may pursue individual ends.[8] For Renouvier, however, man is not so much the "little world" as he is the sum of the whole world; for when one reflects upon the fact that of all that man can know, the foundation and means is in himself,

---

[1] *Introduction to Philosophy* (Eng. transl., by F. Thilly, New York, 1895), pp. 107, ff. F. H. Bradley says "Every fragment of visible Nature might, so far as is known, serve as part in some organism not like our bodies. . . . It is natural to refer to Fechner's vigorous advocacy" (*Appearance and Reality*, London, 1893, p. 271 and n.).

[2] Paulsen, *Introduction*, pp. 109, 233, ff.

[3] *La nouvelle monadologie* (Paris, 1899), pp. 5, 11.

[4] *Ibid.*, p. 11.        [5] *Ibid.*, p. 12.

[6] *Ibid.*, p. 48.        [7] *Ibid.*, p. 46.

[8] *Ibid.*, pp. 326–327.

one will be prepared to admit that, except for God, the creation of the world is primarily and essentially the creation of man.[1]

4. *Affiliations of Royce with Microcosmic Theories.* No recent efforts to show that the universe is characterized by the processes of a consciousness or mind or will have been more imposing than those of Josiah Royce. He advanced as a hypothesis the view that in the case of nature in general, as in the case of the particular portions of nature known as our fellow men, we are dealing with phenomenal signs of a vast conscious process, whose relation to time varies vastly, but whose general characteristics are throughout the same.[2] He thought that

> "This conception of the natural order as a vast social organism of which human society is only a part, is founded upon no merely animistic analogies between the physical phenomena and the phenomena of our organisms, but upon a deeper analogy of the very nature of our conception of other finite beings besides ourselves." [3]

Concerning the nature of this latter conception, he attempts to establish the idealistic thesis that one is conscious of one's Ego only by virtue of the contrast between this Ego and something which one regards as external to one's self, and, in part at least, as an experience possible for one's self rather than actual; but anything that is called experience, even though it be only possible for one's self, must be actual for some other consciousness. There is, therefore, a universe of other actual experience beside one's own finite experience.[4]

> "The whole universe exhibits the phenomenon, first, of one great consciousness, embracing an infinitude of geometrical, physical, chemical, physiological facts; and, secondly, of a vast multitude of individual conscious beings. . . . " [5]

The processes of what is usually regarded as unconscious nature are found to share with those of conscious nature in the narrower sense four

---

[1] *La nouvelle monadologie*, p. 465. A view quite the opposite of this, involving the use of the term microcosm in an epistemological sense, is that of M. Guyau, in *The Non-Religion of the Future* (Eng. transl., New York, 1888), p. 481. "We are obliged to admit the hypothesis of a multitude of microcosms, of mine, yours, everybody's, and of a single macrocosm, the same for everybody. Between the great world and every little world there is an incessant communication. We live in the universe, and the universe lives in us."

[2] *The World and the Individual*, second series (New York, 1908), pp. 226–228; *cf.* pp. 141, 142.

[3] *Studies in Good and Evil* (New York, 1899), p. 207.      [4] *Ibid.*, pp. 207–218.

[5] *The Religious Aspect of Philosophy* (Boston and New York, 1885), p. 349.

features—first, both regions are subject to some condition that demands the irreversibility of great numbers of their processes; second, both regions are subject to processes which involve in general a tendency of one part to communicate, as it were, with another part, influencing what has occurred in one place through what has occurred at another place. This is seen in communications between minds, with attendant assimilations—processes which are similar to, and continuous with, certain still more vast and pervasive series of processes, described as wave-movements. The third feature of resemblance is that "both the material and the mental worlds show a tendency, under favorable conditions, to the appearance of processes resembling those which, in the life of a mind, we call habits." Physical nature is full of at least approximate rhythms; a given process tends to repeat itself over and over, but is often checked by processes of irreversible change. Habits are just such tendencies to routine, to rhythm, in conscious life. Like the rhythms of external nature, they arise, last awhile, and seem to pass away; and the difference between the two series may be chiefly a difference of time-span. The fourth class of processes apparently common to conscious and unconscious nature alike are the processes of evolution.[1] In the evolution of new forms of consciousness (*i.e.*, new biological species), and of new sorts of plans and ideas, there are resemblances. The process of sexual reproduction is regarded as analogous to that of conscious imitation, in which the conscious union of former types of activity results in a new act intermediate between them. In both series, further, there are processes of trial and error, and survival as a result of selection.[2]

In the "Supplementary Essay" of *The World and the Individual*, Royce presents an elaborate argument to show that the Absolute is self-representing. He first adopts Dedekind's theory of an infinite series of numbers as a system that can be exactly represented or imaged, element for element, by one of its own constituent parts.[3] Self-representation is thus taken as a genetic principle of the number system, which system is regarded as having, in barest and most abstract outline, the form of a completed self.[4] It is then declared that any work of the intellect, since it is interpretable in terms of the ordinal numbers, or of some higher type of order, has the structure of a self-representative system.[5] But the

[1] *World and Individual*, second series, pp. 219–223.
[2] *Ibid.*, pp. 315 ff.
[3] *World and Individual*, first series, (1900), pp. 507, ff.
[4] *Ibid.*, p. 534.     [5] *Ibid.*, pp. 535–538.

world itself, in accordance with Royce's "fourth conception of being" is then said to be interpretable in the same way; hence the Absolute must have the form of a Self.[1] The larger Self permits the included self in some aspect of its nature to become an individual and an image of the Absolute.[2] At the same time, society is also an organism, and a fragment of a larger whole;[3] and there may be even a race-consciousness of which individual consciousnesses, animal or human, represent temporally brief sections.[4] Thus, while Royce does not use the term microcosm, his views have a number of points in common with microcosmic theories.

5. *Some More Explicit Microcosmic Theories among the Idealists.* R. B. Perry has defined idealism as "a form of spiritualism in which man the finite individual is regarded as a microcosmic representation of God the absolute reality."[5] Some of the idealists have been more explicit than Royce in aligning themselves with one form or another of microcosmic theory. R. Eucken maintains that when a man attains the spiritual life, "two worlds meet together in him . . . not merely in such a manner that he provides the place in which they meet, but so that he acquires an independent participation in the new world." Whereas in his previous way of living he had been "a mere part of a world," he now becomes "a world in himself, something more than human, something cosmic."[6] Bosanquet says that

"We are minds, living microcosms, not with hard and fast limits, discontinuous with others or with the perfect experience. . . . Nature is complementary to mind, an external system, continuous with our mind, through which the content and purposes of the universe are communicated. The detail of the universe is elicited into mental foci and external conditions pass through them into the complete experience which we call the whole, the Absolute."[7]

A. Seth Pringle-Pattison holds that "every individual is a unique nature, a little world of content, which, as to its ingredients, the tempering of the elements and the systematic structure of the whole, constitutes an expression or focalization of the universe which is nowhere exactly

[1] *World and Individual*, first series, (1900), pp. 544–545.
[2] Second series, p. 303.
[3] *Ibid.*, p. 183.
[4] *Ibid.*, p. 232.
[5] *Present Philosophical Tendencies* (New York, 1912), p. 113.
[6] *Life's Basis and Life's Ideal* (Eng. transl. by A. Widgery, London, 1911), pp. 149–150.
[7] *The Principle of Individuality and Value* (London, 1912), pp. xxxi, xxxvi.

repeated." [1]   As an idealist in the field of philosophy of religion, A. M. Fairbairn holds that the key of all mysteries is man—"what are we but symbols and parables of the vaster life of the whole?"   He thinks that in Christian theology there should be a doctrine of Christ which would "show Him in relation to the whole system of things," and that this is found when the conception of Christ is related to history as the idea of God is related to nature—each is in its own sphere the factor of order, or the condition of a rational system.   Thus the Incarnation is viewed as the epitome and mirror of all the mysteries of being.[2]

*6. Bergson's Doctrine that Organisms Imitate the Universe.*   One of the most important microcosmic conceptions of recent years is that of Bergson, when he compares the living organisms to the universe.

"We do not question the fundamental identity of inert matter and organized matter.   The only question is whether the natural systems which we call living beings must be assimilated to the artificial systems that science cuts out within inert matter, or whether they must not rather be compared to that natural system which is the whole of the universe.   That life is a kind of mechanism I cordially agree.   But is it the mechanism of parts artificially isolated within the whole of the universe, or is it the mechanism of the real whole?" [3]

Bergson thinks that the evolution of living species within a world represents what persists of the original " upward" trend of spirit, as opposed to the downward trend of matter; [4] life on our planet is directed the same way as the creative evolution of the universe; [5] the living forms are "systems which within the whole seem to take after it." [6]

---

[1] *The Idea of God in Recent Philosophy* (Oxford, 1917), p. 267. J. Ward (*Naturalism and Agnosticism*, New York, 1899, vol. I, p. 26) uses the term microcosm in describing the view of some of his opponents, to the effect that our finite knowledge might be so related to the whole as to be, in spite of its finiteness, adequate. J. S. Mackenzie (*Introd. to Social Philos.*, New York, 1895) says that to be rational or self-conscious means to be a microcosm (p. 257; *cf.* pp. 201–202, and p. 184).

[2] *The Philosophy of the Christian Religion* (New York, 1903), pp. 17–18, 60, 478.

[3] *Creative Evolution* (Eng. transl. by Mitchell, New York, 1916), p. 30.

[4] *Ibid.*, p. 247.          [5] *Ibid.*, p. 343.

[6] *Ibid.*, p. 37.   J. E. Boodin in his *Cosmic Evolution* (in *Proc. Arist. Soc.*, vol. XXI, p. 108, 1921), suggests that the life process may imitate the order of the larger cosmos. Bergson's attempt to delineate "a genesis of intellect at the same time as a genesis of material bodies," and to show that intellectuality and materiality have been constituted in detail by reciprocal adaptation (*Creative Evolution*, pp. 186–187) may be interpreted microcosmically. He uses the term microcosm once (p. 214) to designate an artificial system isolated within the world.

*7. Present Emphasis upon Differences between Universe and Man.*
There is in contemporary philosophy a marked tendency to emphasize
differences rather than resemblances between the universe and man; but
sometimes these views are phrased in such a way that they suggest points
of contact with microcosmic theories. This may be illustrated by some
passages from G. Santayana's *Life of Reason:*

> "Like all animals and plants, the cosmos has its own way of doing
> things. . . . Great is this organism of mud and fire, terrible this vast,
> painful, glorious experiment. . . . Why should we not look on the
> universe with piety? . . . Society is not impossible between it and
> us; since it is the source of all our energies. . . shall we not cling to
> it and praise it, seeing that it vegetates so grandly and so sadly?" [1]

Writing in a vein less metaphorical he says of "Nature and Human
Nature":

> "Man is a part of nature and her organization may be regarded as
> the foundation of his own; the word nature is therefore less equivocal
> than it seems, for every nature is Nature herself in one of her more
> specific and better articulated forms. Man therefore represents the
> universe that sustains him; his existence is a proof that the cosmic
> equilibrium that fosters his life is a natural equilibrium, capable of
> being long maintained." [2]

But while the universe thus constitutes the natural basis, man is
charged with the ideal fulfilment—"the Life of Reason is no fair reproduction of the universe, but the expression of man alone." [3] A similar
tendency to interpret nature and man in terms of continuity but to
emphasize the differences between them is to be noted in the work of
F. C. S. Schiller, who thinks that

> "We need not shrink from words like hylozoism or panpsychism,
> provided they stand for interpretations of the lower in terms of the
> higher. For at bottom they are merely forms of Humanism—
> attempts to make the human and the cosmic more akin and to
> bring them closer to us that we may act upon them more success-
> fully." [4]

From a point of view otherwise quite different from those of the
authors just cited, E. G. Spaulding develops the conception of a "creative

---

[1] *Reason in Religion* (New York, 1905), pp. 190-191; *cf.* pp. 192, 249.
[2] *Reason in Common Sense* (New York, 1905), p. 288.
[3] *Reason in Society* (New York, 1905), p. 199.
[4] *Studies in Humanism* (New York, 1907), p. 443.

synthesis" linking nature and human nature, but introducing successive differences between them:

"The atom differs from the electron that composes it—the molecule from its constituent atoms—the cell from its molecules and colloidal particles, society from the human individuals which are its units. No realm of fact, whether subsistent or existent, is exempt from this principle of creative synthesis, in accordance with which one or more specific organizing relations so relate parts that there are new qualities in the resulting whole, and whole and part belong to specifically different universes of discourse. The realm of values is no exception." [1]

8. *Traces of Microcosmic Theory in Sheldon's "Productive Duality."* One contemporary writer finds resemblances between various portions of reality which may, when more fully worked out, lead to some kind of microcosmic theory; this is W. H. Sheldon, in his *Strife of Systems and Productive Duality.* He finds that

"throughout the range of human thought and deed there recurs . . . one and the same problem, viz., to maintain the integrity of a given thing, person, principle, institution, in the modifications which the environment imposes upon it. In the dialect of technical philosophy this is called harmonizing the principle of external relations with that of internal relations." [2]

He presents a solution of the problem, declaring that "the doctrine that one entity cannot be influenced by another without losing its self-identity is pure superstition." [3] Reality is characterized by duality more deeply than by unity. [4] Accordingly, his work

"maps reality as a collection of dyads, or two-in-one monads: if a physical comparison is allowed, of two-atom molecules; if a biological one, of families, each of which is based upon the contrast of sex. It does not at present offer any further chart; it is here limited to the study of the microcosm rather than the macrocosm." [5]

But he thinks the principle will "explain more of the structure of reality than the present volume can show"; [6] what he aims to discover is "something of the plan of the whole universe." [7]

[1] *The New Rationalism* (New York, 1918), p. 500. Spaulding says (p.205) "Does not science . . . picture both the macrocosmically great and the microcosmically small?"

[2] *Strife of Systems* . . . (Cambridge, 1918), p. iii.    [3] *Ibid.*, p. 460.
[4] *Ibid.*, p. 475.    [5] *Ibid.*, p. 524.    [6] *Ibid.*, p. iv.    [7] *Ibid.*, p. 18.

7. SUMMARY: TRACES OF MICROCOSMIC THEORIES IN RECENT SCIENCE
AND PHILOSOPHY

The topics treated in this chapter are indicated in the opening section. In the matter of microcosmic theories in science, it has been noted that the various theories of recapitulation and the organismic theories of society are involved in some difficulties; but that quite recently a number of authorities in different sciences have been interpreting their subject matter in terms drawn from other sciences. Some of these analogies are so striking that they may indicate similarities of structure and process such as would fall under our general definition of microcosmic theories; but few of them are worked out with anything like this in mind. In recent and contemporary philosophy, microcosmic theories are more prominent among the idealists than in the other schools. There is a strong tendency to emphasize not resemblances, but differences between the universe and man. There are indications that as the work of Sheldon is further developed it may present something in the nature of a microcosmic view of the relations of various portions of reality.

# CHAPTER VI

## CONCLUSION: GENERAL ESTIMATE OF MICROCOSMIC THEORIES

### 1. GENERAL SURVEY OF THE HISTORY OF MICROCOSMIC THEORIES

*1. Diversity of Theories Considered, and Their Unity.* We have traced the appearance and development of a large number of theories which have in common the notion that portions of the universe which vary in size exhibit marked resemblances in some of their structures and processes. Often the theories which we have considered seem to have little else in common; and in the different sources they are found along with many differing implications which we have neither precisely excluded nor studied in detail. But between the theories which we have considered we find in most cases, serving as additional threads of connection, either the peculiar microcosmic terminology, or else allusions, general or specific, to the works of other writers, or again the fact that the writers have belonged in the same theological or philosophical tradition. The differences are so great that it would not be correct to speak of "the microcosmic theory," in any save a restricted sense; but on the other hand the resemblances are such that, keeping carefully to the plurals, one may speak of "theories of macrocosms and microcosms."

*2. Widespread Occurrences of these Theories.* Traces of these theories are, as we have shown, found throughout practically the whole history of philosophy, from what are probably meant as references to them among the Pre-Platonic Greeks to a number of diversified views and usages of writers of the present day. Summaries covering the developments indicated are to be found above in connection with each chapter. A general summary such as is now to be attempted might well begin by saying that, although they exhibit periods of rise and decline, such views apparently belong among the philosophical perennials.

*3. Philosophies Unfavorable to Microcosmic Theories.* It is significant to note, although any statement about them must be made in a very general way, the points of contact and opposition which, historically considered, the theories of macrocosms and microcosms are found to exhibit. Beginning with the oppositions, it may be observed that in ancient philosophy such theories are, so far as the evidence goes, almost or quite absent from the works of the Eleatics, Sophists, Epicureans, and Skeptics, and are barely mentioned by Aristotle. They are present but not prominent in the writings of many Christian theologians throughout the mediæval period. They disappear almost entirely in the period dominated by the critical philosophy. They reappear in objective idealism, but in the present period of ascendancy of empiricism and humanism they tend to be disregarded. The microcosmic theories do not flourish in an atmosphere of abstract speculation; they decline when the problem of knowledge is made a difficulty, as well as when interest in the supernatural on the one hand or the humanistic on the other upsets the balance of a consideration more evenly divided between man and the universe; and the theories are likely to be suspected or forgotten in a period when the data of the sciences accumulate faster than they can be organized.

*4. Philosophies Favorable to Microcosmic Theories.* The philosophies apparently most favorable to microcosmic theories have been, in chronological order, hylozoism, Pythagoreanism, probably Stoicism, the work of Philo, Neo-Platonism, the mediæval Jewish philosophy and the *Encyclopædia* of the Arabian Brethren of Sincerity, the work of Paracelsus, Boehme, Leibnitz, Schelling, Schleiermacher, Schopenhauer, Fechner, and the recent absolute idealists. When this group is compared with the group surveyed above it may be said, again in a very general way, that where the microcosmic theories appear the tendency is toward concrete, as distinguished from abstract speculation—toward a speculation which emphasizes a mutual interaction between the universe and man and tries to interpret the one in terms of the other.

*5. Motivations of Microcosmic Theories.* When the history of the theories is surveyed from the point of view of motivations, it appears that the microcosmic interpretations of the universe are associated with all the chief types of value. They may be expressions of either metaphysical, religious, ethical, noetic, or æsthetic interests; or, as most often occurs, may combine something of several or of all these. Sometimes the emphasis is upon a theory of reality which exhibits similarities throughout its various portions. Sometimes, again, it is upon a kinship between man and the universe, or some power thought to be behind the universe. Sometimes the microcosmic theories have urged man to a type of conduct which may be called universal, or cosmic, and have tried to see men's social organizations in terms of larger correspondences.

Again, the theories have served as means to relatively easy generaliza-tions about the world, and to the unifications of such knowledge as the different periods have afforded. And finally, the theories have helped to suggest the beauty of the world and the sublimity of man's possibilities within it—it is not without significance that the term microcosm has been used so much in literature, nor that the word cosmos itself, to one trained in the Greek meanings, connotes beauty as well as order. All these motivations are deep-seated and persistent; and a discussion of the present value of the microcosmic theories may proceed from this point.

6. *Affiliations which Microcosmic Theories have Survived.* Before considering these motivations at the present time it may be noted that in the past, taken singly or together, and measured from one period of the history of philosophy to another, they have been strong enough to bring the microcosmic theories through their temporary affiliations with the ancient mythologies, the fatalism of the Stoics, the fantastic analogies of the mediæval Jews and Arabs, the vagaries of astrology and alchemy, and the irresponsible speculations of a Schellingian philosophy of nature. These matters are no longer to be charged against the microcosmic theories, because the latter have shown themselves able to survive them, and exhibit vitality in new forms.

7. *Affiliations Which Still Afford Ground for Criticism.* It must, how-ever, be added that to many at the present time the microcosmic theories still seem to be involved in some of their early modern and more recent affiliations—in a mysticism like that of Boehme, or a panpsychism like that of Fechner, or an over-confident idealism like that of Lotze, or a block universe like that of Royce, or an ill-conceived scientific adventure like the theories of recapitulation and the organismic theories of society, or, in general, an unwarranted dependence upon the insecure method of analogy. The problem of the present value of the microcosmic theories depends then upon the strength of the motivations which make for them and the evidence which supports them, measured against the strength of such criticisms as these.

## 2. THE PRESENT VALUE OF MICROCOSMIC THEORIES

*1. Criticisms at Present Forcing Modifications of Theories.* There is no question that according to the current estimate criticisms such as those just mentioned are too strong for the microcosmic theories, and are making necessary decided modifications of them as the price of their retention. In this section an attempt will be made, first, to indicate modified types of microcosmic theories which are or may be widely accepted at the present time, as implications or even as equivalents of views already prevalent. Thus we shall consider the possible significance of microcosmic theories as expressions of æsthetic, noetic, ethical, and religious values, bearing in mind that we are dealing with expressions in regard to which there may be, not merely individual acceptance here and there, but rather general agreement. After having examined these restatements one by one, we shall then try to estimate their combined significance. Finally, in a concluding paragraph, we shall indicate briefly a metaphysical position which, if it were adopted, might render possible a restatement of microcosmic theories from another point of view.

2. *Present Æsthetic Value of Microcosmic Theories.* Of the persistent motivations which may be expected to keep the microcosmic theories reappearing, there need be no question that the æsthetic motivation has possibilities which are at once the most abundant and the least explored. They are abundant because the realm of æsthetics is so broad and fair, so largely free from the restraints imposed by the world of facts. In æsthetic creation one may disregard and even contradict the evidence drawn from all realms less colorful. Now, since recent years have witnessed such a marked renaissance of the imagination in philosophy, it may be that at some no very distant time the philosophical imagination as such will be turned, in a way which all will recognize as legitimate, upon the physical universe, as well as upon man and his affairs. It does not seem very likely, because the prestige of the natural sciences is now so overwhelming; but if the time ever comes it is possible that the successive complicated repetitions of pattern according to some microcosmic theory may, like the chords of a Pythagorean lyre, or the recurrent motif of a Schopenhauerian symphony, appeal to imaginations eager to catch a strain of what the ancients felt to be the cosmic harmonies. This is, as was said, a field practically unexplored; but certainly somewhere in it there is something which has gone out of the modern world.

3. *Present Noetic Value of Microcosmic Theories.* Quite different from the foregoing is another aspect of possible significance of the microcosmic theories, upon which there may be general agreement. So far as one can see, it will always be possible, and largely unavoidable, to make a certain epistemological and logical use of them. For, with the growing distrust of false problems in this field, we are being forced to a new recognition of the fact that the account of the world which our minds afford must be

taken as, in the main, and at least potentially, a trustworthy account. If any one cares to insist upon it, this statement can always be made to mean that the mind in some sense of the word tends to represent the world on a small scale, and hence to afford a microcosm of it. So far as one can see, it makes little difference here which of the various theories of knowledge is adopted; but it must also be said that the so-called microcosmic relation here is so universal and so inevitable that it has no conspicuous or particular meaning.

4. *Present Ethical Value of Microcosmic Theories.* The case of ethical values is somewhat more promising. Along with a modification of Darwinism in biology, to the effect that evolution often proceeds by co-operation as well as by the elimination of the unfit, there has come a modification of Huxleyism in ethics, to the effect that the cosmos cannot, after all, be altogether opposed to the presence of man. But, figuratively speaking, in ethics we still approach the cosmos with a good deal of diffidence, fearing lest it cast upon us the shadow of Stoic fatalism, or in some other way set at naught our creative intelligence. This hesitation may be partially overcome if it is recognized that the law of the cosmos itself is creativity—that it proceeds by a creative evolution, or by a series of creative syntheses; perhaps even that it is "creating creators." [1] If this be granted, the microcosmic phraseology may be freely used to urge the cultivation of broad sympathies and manifold attainments; and, outside the realm of religion, few metaphors are more striking than these, with their veritable "world of meaning." Such ideals when upheld go far toward counteracting the excessive specialization which is one of the faults of our time, as well as its other forms of more serious one-sidedness and excess.

5. *Present Religious Value of Microcosmic Theories.* It is as difficult in connection with microcosmic theories as it is in every other respect to secure agreement concerning religious values. According to some current estimates of religion, everything essential has been said when æsthetic and ethical values have been discussed; for religion is regarded as a kind of intermediate stage in their development, as an extension of the ethical or æsthetic interest into the realm of myth and subsistence which issues in new æsthetic or ethical consequences. According to the older views, and to those who accept them in a more or less modified form, existence is itself a capital element in value, and values tend to evaporate unless they have existential sources and sanctions. Since in this section we

[1] Phrase used by E. W. Lyman, in another connection.

are noting possible agreements, it may be said here that there is one point in which these contending views seem to be just beginning to blend—it is in the attachment of a higher religious value to the physical universe. If the manifold difficulties of such a compromise measure can be overcome it may afford an object of religion which is at once spacious enough for the creative imagination and reliable enough for the spiritual experience; we may, in Santayana's phrase, regard the universe with piety, and experience what Clifford called cosmic emotion. But it is evident that, according to the opinions at present most widespread, such a consummation would contain a preponderant admixture of the imaginative element; and the same would be true of any microcosmic theories modelled upon it. So far as present opinions go, then, there would be here no advance upon the situation noted in the cases of æsthetic and ethical values.

6. *Summary of these Estimates of Microcosmic Theories.* The foregoing estimates of the microcosmic theories may be summed up by saying that, from the point of view at present prevailing, the æsthetic interpretation of microcosmic theories is too far-fetched; the epistemological interpretation is too self-evident; the ethical interpretation is powerful, but its power is that of a metaphor rather than that of a fact; and the religious interpretation draws so heavily upon the imagination that it loses its claim to literal truth. On the whole, then, it might seem to be better to leave the microcosmic theories to lie like fossils scattered throughout the upheaved and faulting strata of the history of philosophy, than to try to breathe into them the breath of life.

7. *Indications of Recrudescence of Microcosmic Theories.* Yet if the past is to teach us anything it should be to remember that in studying the microcosmic theories we are dealing with a philosophical perennial—or to keep the other figure, with a species which is remarkably persistent. In the strata of the history of philosophy which are even now being laid down there are scattering indications of the vitality of some notions which may be called microcosmic. It may be said that they exhibit vitality, because they occur in connection with some of the most flourishing portions of contemporary knowledge, namely, the sciences, some of the interpretative analogies of which are indicated in the preceding chapter. The analogies are, as was said, scattered, and uncertain, and uncoördinated; there are, however, enough of them so that from this point of view the suggestion presents itself that if the world could be interpreted in terms of a concrete and realistic monadism whose individual units, as studied in laboratories and observatories, are seen in their

interactions with one another to exhibit essentially similar structures and processes, the way might be open for a modern microcosmic view, which, in so far as it was founded upon scientific evidence would not be exposed to some of the criticisms levelled against the views of the past, and which at the same time would be able to modify in the direction of existential sanctions some of the current conceptions of values. The possibility appears to be strengthened when one considers that, with different and doubtless more adequate epistemological presuppositions and with slight changes in his scientific interests, Herbert Spencer might have turned in this direction his data of evolution; and that Bergson, the outstanding critic of the Spencerian conceptions, has himself advanced one or two of the most striking microcosmic hypotheses of our time. It is a question, however, not of the history of the theories, but of the realistic metaphysics, of the logical justification of such a method of analogy as would be necessary, and of the scientific evidences of similarities in structures and processes.[1] These points are in fact all reducible

---

[1] In an article entitled "Evolution and Epitomization" (*Monist.* vol. xxxi, pp. 536–584), I have indicated in a preliminary and tentative way what seem to me to be some possible steps in such an argument. The hypothesis is to the effect that the data of evolution, when studied in detail, may be seen to exhibit also a concomitant process of epitomization—the latter being defined as the repetition, at successive stages of evolution, of structures and processes essentially analogous to those of other stages whose units vary in size. Three implications of this hypothesis are developed in the article—first, that of a realistic monadism, such as is alluded to above. For this, I have taken, with a number of qualifications and indications of difficulties involved, the series: electrons, atoms, molecules, astronomical bodies, solar systems, star clusters, etc., . . .; organic compounds, . . . unicellular organisms, multicellular organisms, social groups . . . ; specialized cells, nervous areas, reflex arcs, complex reflexes, (instinct- and value-) complexes . . . (pp. 541–543). I have treated at some length a portion of the evidence which I think goes to show that each of these monads or members of the series tends to exhibit (I) a relative individuation in a milieu; (II) interactions, especially with monads previously developed, involving accretions and depletions; (III) at least in some cases a process of reproduction of new monads from old; and (IV), again in some cases at least a process of integration or "creative synthesis," accompanied by differentiations of structure, and resulting in the formation of relatively individuated monads (I) of the next stage (pp. 543–572). A consideration of these similarities, as well as of the breaks observable in the series of monads as enumerated above, leads to the formulation of the second implication of epitomization, to the effect that the cosmogonic series, as above enumerated, is epitomized by the biological series, and the biological series, in turn, is epitomized by the neuropsychological (pp. 572–574). A more concrete estimate of this relation leads to the formulation of the third implication, to the effect that the structures and processes studied in ecology are epitomized by those studied in physiological psychology.

to the last-named; for any view that is supported by scientific evidence can if necessary fashion its own logic, and fight its own metaphysical battles. If this should turn out to be the case with a realistic monadism such as is here suggested—or perhaps even, so long as the question of its possibility remains open—the long-neglected microcosmic theories of the past may, in addition to their historical importance and their human interest, have a vicarious meaning and an illustrative function.

The general result of the three implications is a view that the structures and processes of the universe tend, by a kind of progressive concentration throughout the monads of the cosmogonic, biological, and neuropsychological series to be, so to speak, distilled into, or brought to a focus in the social groups and through these into our values and ideas. The universe is viewed as not merely evolving, with the result that men and their experiences have appeared, but also as epitomizing, with the result that men and their experiences have a more significant relation to the whole (p. 582).

# INDEX OF AUTHORS

Numbers refer to pages and notes.   Names of doxographers, editors and translators
are in most cases not included.